Grace Explained

Also by Fr. Brian Mullady, O.P.
from EWTN Publishing:

The Decalogue Decoded

Captivated by the Master

Fr. Brian Thomas Becket Mullady, O.P., S.T.D.

Grace Explained

How to Receive — and Retain — God's Most Potent Gift

EWTN PUBLISHING, INC.

Irondale, Alabama

*To Reginald Martin and Anthony Patalano,
my companions in the Dominican life*

Contents

Grace Explained

Chapter 1

Man Fully Alive

His divine power has granted to us all things that pertain to life and godliness, through the knowledge of him who called us to his own glory and excellence, by which he has granted to us his precious and very great promises, that through these you may escape from the corruption that is in the world because of passion, and become partakers of the divine nature. (2 Pet. 1:3–4)

The theme of this book is grace, because it is by grace that we become partakers of the divine nature. This means God dwelling in our souls so that we can have a life of intimacy with the Holy Trinity—a relationship that brings us to the very level of God Himself.

To understand this beautiful truth, we will have to explore what human nature is, how our nature is called to a relationship with God, and what that relationship with God looks like. We will also look at how revelation and faith fit into that call, and finally how grace fits in: what causes grace, who is the author of grace, what grace is, what it means to be justified by grace, and how, by grace, we can merit the rewards of Heaven.

But we're going to begin by examining the modern errors that make understanding all this very difficult. In the last century, the idea has become dominant that man is the captain of his fate and the master of his soul, such that it makes him in some way *less human* to rely upon any power higher than himself—including grace.

Let's start with something we all recognize. In the sixties, it was very popular to hang felt banners in churches. (I know it still is in some places.) And one of the most popular sayings people used to write on those banners was this: "The glory of God is man fully alive." This is a real quotation, and it comes from a great Father of the Church, St. Irenaeus.

But the people who made these banners didn't write the second half of the quotation, and that second half makes all the difference in the world. Here is the full statement of St. Irenaeus: "The glory of God is man fully alive, and *the life of man is the vision of God*." This shows us that man fully alive *in an earthly sense* is not what God is primarily interested in. Rather, for a man to be fully alive he has to surrender himself to, and have a relationship with, a being who is higher and deeper than himself—something he cannot do by his own power. Further, this means that the fullness of human life is never finally experienced here. So many people today think we can establish a human utopia here on earth, as though if we had the most perfect government we would be in Heaven.

Rather, what St. Irenaeus emphasizes is that this life is only a pilgrimage. It's a preparation for our final resting place, which is to know and to love God as He is in Himself—something not possible by our own weak human power. Man left to himself is man imperfect and frustrated. Only when we are elevated to God—only when we are raised into His own inner life—is it possible for us to finally be at peace, to experience a final and full reconciliation with ourselves, with the world, and with God. In other words, loving intimacy with God is what human life is made for. Death isn't the final end. And so, here on earth, we must take every step not just from our own human point of view toward the world, but from God's point of view.

One of my favorite images of what human life should be like is the painting *Christ of St. John of the Cross*, by Salvador Dalí. The point of view of the painting is from above a huge, crucified Christ, looking down with Him from the Cross at our tiny little world. We can only really understand and appreciate the reality of human life when we adopt the supernatural point of view, looking down on all of time and all of space. And it is grace that gives us the ability to do this.

In the modern world, however, we find the idea of a supernatural view of life — one that is distant but also, through grace, intimate — impossible to comprehend. This comes first from a collapsing of the distinction between humanity and the rest of creation, where we see creation itself as containing God or as our path to maintaining intimacy with Him. In the past four hundred years especially, we have suffered from a very peculiar philosophy of creation's relationship to God. And since human beings are a part of creation, this can't but affect the way we look at our own fulfillment.

Sir Isaac Newton looked upon the world as an ideal set of physical laws that sprang from the mind of the Creator, with no further need on the part of that Creator to help them become more perfect. Now we know today, of course, following Albert Einstein, that Newton's physics is imperfect, but his way of viewing things has stuck in the modern consciousness. We think that everything should conform to certain ideal mathematical laws of motion, as if the Creator God perfectly kicked a perfect football into the void, then went on His way. According to this view, any attempt to raise this football-creation beyond itself would mean that the kicker was somehow imperfect. Thus, any attempt to interfere with the laws of nature somehow made God less God, and creation less creation. All humans could do is try to find the perfection that the Creator had placed in nature.

In this view of creation, there's no room for a power that raises us beyond what we are already by creation; that is, there's no room for grace. Human reason becomes the only sign of God we can find in the world—and so man, in a sense, becomes God. To say that there's some supernatural truth to which I have to conform myself—a Trinity for example—or to say that religion demands that I lose myself in order to find myself, these ideas are thought to do a kind of injustice to the primordial perfection of God's creation.

The second modern error is in a sense the opposite, but also very much like it, because extremes in thought often touch each other, like the ends of a horseshoe converging. If the first error was characteristic of the rationalists of the seventeenth and eighteenth centuries, the second was a reaction to this cold and detached way of looking at God. In this error, God is made identical with the world. The philosopher Benedict de Spinoza is the person who most characteristically expressed this way of looking at things. For him, God was the same as his emotions and the human desire for perfection. We see something similar in the New Age movement, which asks us to find God within ourselves.

Others said that theology was anthropology, i.e., that the study of God was the study of man and his powers. This culminated in Friedrich Nietzsche, who said that if God is just a projection of ourselves that keeps us from reaching our full potential, why not dispense with Him entirely? That is, in order to find out what it means to be truly human, we have to dispense with the idea that there is some higher being than man.

Catholicism affirms neither of these extremes. We read at the very beginning of Scripture:

In the beginning God created the heavens and the earth. The earth was without form and void, and darkness was upon the face of the deep; and the Spirit of God was moving over the face of the waters. (Gen. 1:1–2)

Who is the beginning, the foundation stone that underscores and underlies every part of creation? This beginning is the same wisdom that underlies all of time, from which time came forth and to which time is ordered.

> In the beginning was the Word, and the Word was with God, and the Word was God. He was in the beginning with God; all things were made through him, and without him was not anything made that was made. (John 1:1–3)

We can almost say that the foundation of all of time, from which it comes forth and to which it is returning, is *intimacy with God* and not just God Himself: The relationship of the Blessed Trinity is the basis and the foundation of everything that is — and yet He is not the same as everything that is. That is, God is intrinsic to the world and intimate to the world but not identical with the world; and at the same time He is outside of the world, but not extrinsic to or disinterested in the world. That is, He is transcendent from this changeable realm, but since He created it, His intrinsic presence in each thing and being is necessary for it to continue acting according to its nature. So God is intimate to everything, but as its *cause*, not as a *part* of its being. God, by His power, supports everything that exists, and especially He supports it in bringing it back to Himself, as it comes forth from Him and desires to return to Him.

In order to really understand the relationship between God and creation, we also need to consider the Trinity. Our understanding of the Trinity today is very weak. On Trinity Sunday, too often priests just tell the people that the Trinity is just an unintelligible mystery that has nothing to do with daily life and ethics. But we are baptized in the name of the Trinity, confirmed in the name of the Trinity, married in the name of the Trinity, and anointed in the name of the Trinity! Jesus spoke in the name of the Trinity! And still we feel like we can't say anything at all about our triune God.

This is a terrible shame, because we can see the perfection of the intimacy to which we are called to with God *within God* among the Father, the Son, and the Holy Spirit.

When we say that this is irrelevant to everyday life, we lose sight of the very foundation of our faith, our nature, and our dignity. Let's look at the dignity of man as proclaimed in Genesis, after the creation of the world in the intimacy of the Trinity—a creation that is supported in an ongoing way by His love and power: "Let us make man in our image, after our likeness.... So God created man in his own image, in the image of God he created him; male and female he created them" (1:26–27). Then, in Genesis 2, we read that "God formed man of dust from the ground, and breathed into his nostrils the breath of life" (2:7). This "breath of life," was God Himself, which grants us a Trinitarian likeness to God.

This means that we have the mind, will, and spirit to arrive at intimacy with God in a way that no other part of creation does. How do we do this? We certainly can't arrive at it by our own power. The Scriptures tell us God made man right, and Jesus tells us what it means to be made right after His coming: "Holy Father, keep them in thy name, which thou hast given me, that they may be one, even as we are one" (John 17:11). Jesus wants us to share in the very unity of the Trinity. In this, Christ calls us back to the original perfection of Adam, before his Original Sin, when he was able to know and love God not just as his Creator but as his friend; he was able to participate in God's peace.

God created man with a special aid to his being, a special interior change by which man walked and talked in intimacy with God in the garden, and by which he knew God's ways as his own. The classical theologians say that Adam experienced the continuous state of infused contemplation by grace, and in this sense he was able to prepare *himself* for Heaven. We will explore throughout this book how grace works in our life to return us to that perfection, without the direct, personal access to God that Adam had.

St. Paul wrote to the Colossians, "If then you have been raised with Christ, seek the things that are above, where Christ is, seated at the right hand of God" (3:1). This experience, this striving to seek God with His help, is not an alienation of our nature, but its fulfillment. Intimacy with God is man's highest calling, which we can achieve by relying upon God's sanctifying grace, which makes us holy. This is how we discover what it means to be truly human, because the glory of God is man fully alive, but the life of man is the vision of God.

Chapter 2

The Meaning of Life

In this chapter, we will discuss the purpose of human life, how we can see this purpose reflected in both Scripture and Tradition, and how this purpose is rooted in human nature.

We read in the book of Psalms:

> How lovely is thy dwelling place,
> O LORD of hosts!
> My soul longs, yea, faints
> for the courts of the Lord;
> my heart and flesh sing for joy
> to the living God. (Ps. 84:1–2)

> O God, thou art my God, I seek thee,
> my soul thirsts for thee;
> my flesh faints for thee,
> as in a dry and weary land where no water is.
> So I have looked upon thee in the sanctuary,
> beholding thy power and glory.
> Because thy steadfast love is better than life,
> my lips will praise thee.
> So I will bless thee as long as I live;
> I will lift up my hands and call on thy name.
>   (Ps. 63:1–4)

Grace Explained

What else can this mean but that our souls, and that human nature itself, have a need for God? But what kind of knowledge of God is it that we are yearning for? How does this relate to the things that compose us as human beings, in body and soul? Is this just something that God zapped into us as individuals? Is it something that we were given over time in God's plan for us? Or is it something that God instilled in us by the very way that our bodies relate to our souls, and our souls relate to God?

Let's examine human powers. Man is like a pyramid or a hierarchy of types of powers. The first and most basic are the "vegetative powers" of living beings—we take in food, sunlight, water, and so on, and use them to build living tissue. Man also has powers that he shares with the animals, which we call sensitive powers. These aren't just the five senses, but also the inner sense or ability to organize perceptions and recognize a tree, for instance, and distinguish it from, say, a chair. Man also has the ability to move himself toward something that he enjoys—the power of sensible love—and the ability to flee from something he doesn't enjoy—the power of sensible hate.

Being made in the image and likeness of God, however, makes man special among all the creatures in the world. There are two things in chapter two of Genesis that God presents to man to show him that he is different from all the rest of the creatures. First of all, God brings the animals to man to be named. To give a name to something, in the ancient Hebrew understanding, means that a person understands the nature of that thing totally—that he cannot just describe it or its characteristics but can have a true appreciation of its inner being. Thus man shows that he has the ability not only to sensibly describe the difference between a horse and a goat but also to understand their inner constitution, to be able to define them. In other words, man has self-awareness, self-consciousness, and intellect. This is not just because the human brain is more organized or more complete than in animals; it's because he has something special about him from being made in the image of God.

The second thing God does is enable man to cooperate in realizing his destiny. All the other things God has made—the plants, the animals, the rocks, the sun, the moon, and the stars—have no choice about whether to fulfill their purposes. But man may or may not cooperate in realizing his destiny. God implicitly places a commandment before him: You are going to show that you are above and beyond all the other beings that exist because you will choose my love and my intimacy; you will choose to act according to the nature of the world and the universe and yourself. In other words, man has a free will. So we really have three kinds of powers: those we share with organic matter, those we share with animals, and those—the intellect and the will—that we share with the angels. "Thou didst make him for a little while lower than the angels, thou hast crowned him with glory and honor" (Heb. 2:7, referencing Ps. 8:5).

What can fulfill these powers of the human soul? You know, people put their happiness in all kinds of things—food and drink, power, money, pleasure—as if any one of them can completely fulfill the soul. And if human powers were limited to those of a vegetable or sensitive animal, they wouldn't "be wrong." But man has an intelligence, and anything that does not fulfill the intelligence cannot fulfill his complete nature. What, then, fulfills the intellect?

The first time a person understands why something exists, he's filled with wonder at the order of reason. And so he wants to progress further and further in that wonder. Once a person begins to understand the reasonability of the world, he can never stop—that wonder can never be fulfilled—until he experiences the primal explanation, the first *why*. And this cannot happen until he knows the ordering mind who created and organized the universe. Therefore, until we see the Trinity face-to-face in Heaven, we cannot be perfect, and our desire for truth and goodness cannot be finally fulfilled.

What a wonderful doctrine this is: It means that we were made for Heaven! As St. Augustine famously said, "You have made us for Yourself, O Lord, and our heart is restless until it rests in You." What does this resting mean? In the final analysis, it means resting in God, and yet we cannot even move ourselves one pace toward Heaven without God's power, because God is so infinite that we cannot bring ourselves beyond this world: We have to be led there. We have to be given the strength. Adam was created in grace, so he could do it, but everyone since cannot.

And so the truth is that man is called by nature to see God. This is a primary and foundational truth of Christianity. It's also the source of the truth that grace does not alienate man from his nature, but rather fulfills that nature. It's not possible for human beings to really be human without the vision of God. Therefore, there can be no true secular humanism because this rules out the divine indwelling of the Holy Trinity; it rules out knowing as God knows and loving as God loves.

This has become a difficulty today because there's a trend to deny the distinction between the natural and supernatural orders, between grace and nature, between God in Himself and creation. This causes a problem because grace perfects nature, and so it must not be the same as nature, and it certainly does not destroy it. Man is only perfect when he possesses grace and so only fully human and free; the failure to distinguish nature from grace in an adequate way threatens to unseat this basic truth. There have been two tendencies in explaining the relation of nature to grace, and both have been somewhat inadequate.

The first is a traditional solution that has been around for about five hundred years. It was initiated by a man named Cardinal

Thomas Cajetan, who argued that man was truly ordered to the vision of God—but not by anything in his nature as such. Rather, God gave man an additional grace at creation. In other words, if you examine the human powers we have described, Cajetan's view is that you couldn't find any that demanded the vision of God for its completion; there is nothing, on this account, in our nature *alone* that orders us to Heaven. In fact, people could be happy just knowing that God existed, like the pre-Christian philosophers knew.

What this suggests, however, is that somehow man and his nature can be neutral with respect to God. It says that God zaps into man an additional purpose that's different than the purpose of his powers in themselves. This creates a kind of hybrid human nature—and it makes nature and grace far apart, detaching our natural and supernatural purposes. This leads to ideas like the separation of "secular" politics, which can order life completely without missing anything essential, from the "religious" matters proper to the Church. Cajetan certainly did not mean to teach this, but this has been the result of his theory in modern times.

The other error, which regards human nature as basically undefinable, originates in modern times. This is most closely associated with the theologian Karl Rahner, who said that each man's ordering toward God is individualized and not part of a general human nature. Rahner calls human nature without the vision of God a "remainder concept." That is, if you subtract the vision of God from the complete human nature, you get something real and existing, but about which nothing definitive can be said. Thus he places a wedge between our natural and supernatural ends, creating a kind of undefinable hybrid.

The result has been that either we consider nature and grace to be farther apart than ever, or we collapse the distinction between the two altogether. This is where we get the idea, for instance, that the real purpose and perfection of Holy Mass is the human community coming together and sharing a meal rather than the Sacrifice by which we are elevated to His divine life. We have come, too often, to believe that our this-worldly community is the very same as God's life, instead of being ordered toward a perfection beyond. The relationship between God's supernatural order and the natural order has been clouded over.

The root of both of these errors is something very subtle but very important. When we talk about the desire to see God, most people think of it as a *desire of the will*, which means that it requires a conscious moral decision. Therefore, it can't be there just by nature because that would mean that God is *obliged* to give His supernatural life to human beings, which would compromise His perfect freedom. But in the work of St. Thomas Aquinas, the desire for God is not a desire of the will, but rather is related to the power in man that wonders at the causes of the world, a wonder that can only be satisfied in seeing God. That power, of course, is the intellect, and that is where the desire to see God is located.

Since this tendency is identical with all natures having an intellect, it must be true for the angels as well. Though each angel has its own unique nature, because of the presence of the intellect, their natural fulfillment must be the same as man's. The tendency to the supernatural is not caused by the ability to realize this purpose or to be created in grace; it is identical with possessing an intellect. Thomas gives six arguments for this that have nothing to do with man being created in grace, and nothing to do with the will whatsoever, but rather have to do with the inadequacy of the unaided mind to know the truth — not only for man, but also for angels.

First of all, what is imperfect desires the perfect. The angels know that even with their keen intelligence, their knowledge is imperfect by nature, so even they have to be elevated by grace to desire the vision of God.

Second, ignorance desires to be resolved. The angels, by nature, know their ignorance of God in Himself; therefore, by nature, they know that only when they see God in the face will this ignorance be resolved.

Third, once one knows the effects of a thing, one wants to know its first cause. The angels know perfectly that they are effects of God and they know the philosophical truth of God, certainly much better than we do, but they naturally want to know the final explanation.

Fourth, one who knows *that* something exists wants to know *what the thing is*. The angels know that God exists, but then they want to know who God is.

Fifth, beings which experience intellectual knowledge want to escape ignorance. By nature, angels and men know they are ignorant of who God is as such. This is also true in the knowledge of faith, which is the essence of things unseen and the substance of things to be hoped for (cf. Heb. 11:1). Even those with the certainty of faith know that the more they love God, the more they come to realize they are ignorant of His nature and so they desire to escape this ignorance. St. Paul says, "We now know through a glass darkly, but then we shall know even as we are known face to face" (1 Cor. 13:12).

And finally, the closer something gets to full knowledge, the more it has a passion to complete that knowledge — and in the case of God, to know Him, to be with Him, and to be the same as He is. The angels are more like God than we are by nature, and so they have more of a desire to be like Him through knowing Him as He is in Heaven; man, on the other hand, can be raised by grace to knowing Him completely as He is in Himself. Man is directly created by God. The human soul cannot be created only by a mother and a father because the creative spirit is something that demands God's direct power. If man can only be directly created by God, then only experiencing God directly can satisfy him.

We have to say then that there is in the powers of the human soul a natural desire to see God's face in Heaven. Those who think there is not, or who place the purpose of man in something besides God, suffer a narrowness in their point of view that can only be cured if we admit that the mind itself — its dynamism to know, and its wonder about the causes of the world — can only come to restful fulfillment in seeing God. Human beings and angels also can only arrive at this experience through sanctifying grace in the will.

It is important to note that the desire causes the need for grace, and not the other way around. Man by nature is called to an end he cannot attain by nature because of the exalted character of the end. Thomas Aquinas puts it this way: "Ultimate felicity is to be sought in nothing other than the operation of the intellect, since no desire carries on to such sublime heights as the desire to understand the truth" (*Summa contra Gentiles*, III, 50). Other desires human beings have can be satisfied in other things, but not this one. Aquinas concludes then about the sublimity of human nature: "Let those men be ashamed, then, who seek man's felicity in the most inferior things when it is so highly situated" (*Summa contra Gentiles* III, 50).

Chapter 3

The Knowledge of Faith

In the first chapter, we took up the question of whether it is possible for unaided human reason to come to know the truth in its fullness. The so-called rationalists thought that there was nothing human beings had to know for their fulfillment that they couldn't discover by their reason alone. The Church categorically denies this: Even such a marvelous creature as Adam before his Original Sin, while he had access to the truths of the natural world, needed God's help to discover the fullness of truth toward which the human mind is ordered—the knowledge of God and of the supernatural order, the knowledge God Himself has of the world.

Think of St. Dominic, who used to pray using gestures with his hands; one of his favorite gestures was to point himself to Heaven like an arrow as though his whole self—his body, his emotions, his mind, and his will—could be somehow shot toward God. And when St. Elizabeth of the Trinity entered her convent, she was asked, "Are you sometimes homesick for Heaven?" She replied: "I am sometimes homesick for heaven but except for the vision I possess everything which is in heaven already here on earth, through grace."

In this chapter, other kinds of knowing must be identified as a prelude to discussing the necessity of grace. What other kind of knowledge is necessary for human beings to be perfect, beyond that which can be attained through the senses? Is there another knowledge that is not just icing on the cake—an additional and optional bonus—but that constitutes the core and the fullness of human knowledge itself? As we have said, we are ordered and called to the vision of God. But we experience the beginnings of, and preparation for, that knowledge right here on earth in the form of revelation.

In order for any human being to be really integrated, to be really perfect, reason and science are not enough. Faith is necessary. If it is true that having a loving conversation with God is necessary for the fullness of human nature, then faith, which is the beginning of that conversation here on earth, is also necessary. And revelation, by its very definition, would be the means to faith.

How does faith relate to the different kinds of human knowledge that we can have concerning God? There are four different ways by which a human being knows God. The first is by a kind of intuition. Human beings are not naturally atheists; we have a natural sense that there is a being beyond this world, who is the fullness and the cause of the beings that exist here. The trouble is, though, that this intuition is insufficient to know the true God. While it leads us to say that there has to be some ultimate being, who exactly that ultimate being is depends on our desires or prejudices.

This brings us to a second way of knowing God: by reason. The ancient Greek philosophers, for instance, reasoned to the existence of a single cause, a single Creator. This is described in, among other places, the famous "Five Ways" of St. Thomas Aquinas, by which he shows that it's possible for the human mind to discover not just that God exists but many things about God's nature by examining the world around him. But the truth is that only a few people can get there without error. After the Original Sin, because of the darkness of our minds (see 1 Cor. 13:12), it is very hard to discover even these truths about God; and so God also reveals these truths to us.

Even this, however, is not the final knowledge of God we can have here on earth to prepare ourselves for the fourth kind of knowledge, which is knowledge by vision in Heaven when we will know even as we are known, without any intermediary. God gives us a third kind of knowledge between the knowledge of reason and the knowledge of Heaven, and this is the knowledge of faith. By the knowledge of faith, before the Original Sin, Adam understood the Trinity and the ordering of the world to the Trinity in the manner of God. Neither before nor after Original Sin can we reason to the Trinity by reason alone. This doesn't mean that the Trinity is an unreasonable teaching, but that only through faith in Jesus Christ and the grace of God can we come to see it and embrace it.

There are two truths for which faith in revelation is absolutely necessary, so that the human mind may be enlightened to begin our preparation for Heaven: the fact that God is a Trinity, and the fact that God became man—and therefore our way to the Trinity. Other than that, it's possible for human beings to discover many things about God through reason, but these are inadequate to the mystery. St. Thomas demonstrates, for example, that the same God Whom Plato discovered as the good and Aristotle as the prime mover is the One revealed to Moses on Mount Sinai as "I am who am" (the divine name: *Yahweh*). While the idea of the Creator could be known by reason alone, because of the darkness of our minds from the Original Sin, God still had to reveal Himself, and His name, to us. And the Incarnation and the Trinity absolutely require the further knowledge of faith.

It is no more possible for human beings to be satisfied with merely knowing the existence and attributes of God than it would be for an animal to be satisfied with the life of a plant, or a plant to be satisfied with a life of a rock. Man stands at the top of the pyramidal hierarchy of creation (among the material beings) and can see to the horizon. We can see the clarity of the air and the solidity of the mountains: The mountain is like the body and the air like the spirit. Man himself is not only spirit, nor is he only matter: He is a unique combination of both, so he stands on the horizon of being between flesh and spirit, between time and eternity. If this is true, then it is necessary for human life that we experience a kind of spiritual knowledge which is not open to us simply by the knowledge of the senses. This is the knowledge of faith, the knowledge of revelation.

So marvelous is man that he can be satisfied with nothing less than knowing God as He is in Himself, and so God must condescend to give him a way of knowing that doesn't contradict scientific knowledge. Therefore, Catholics are certainly not against human reason, but rather we celebrate the supplements God gives us that take us out of our worldly box and open us up to the infinite. This is available to every human person, no matter how great or how small, no matter how intelligent or how lacking in intelligence: Every human person, by God's revelation, no matter at what time or in what place they lived, must partake of the divine nature, which we first touch through this knowledge.

Now, of course, the knowledge of faith is imperfect because we do not yet *see* the One in Whom we believe. Indeed, one definition of faith from St. Paul is: "The assurance of things hoped for, the conviction of things not seen" (Heb. 11:1). We believe the words of Christ; we believe the words of God revealed to us; sometimes even we are granted some image or some light directly in our minds. But even so, we don't yet enter directly into the very mystery. The mind still wants to know who God is directly. Here, Christ is our mediator to experience that mystery, and we believe what Christ says because He shows us who He is through the signs of His miracles and fulfilled prophecies.

We have to have a personal relationship with Jesus Himself, so that what He tells us can stimulate our intelligence: we might even call this the science of faith. Faith, of course, is not something that human reason and science can discover; it's something we depend upon God to explain to us. But, once explained, it's perfectly reasonable and compatible with the manner of human knowing—but now, instead of beginning with our sensible experiences to discover the ultimate truth of the world, we begin with God.

This is the difference between philosophical and theological knowledge. Philosophy begins with the world, going out to find the deepest reasons or causes of the natural world. Finding God through that experience is like going out to dig a grave and finding a treasure: sensible things can lead us to their Creator, but with a good deal of difficulty and uncertainty, and even then only for those with the intelligence and time to persevere in the quest. Religious knowledge, however, based on Scripture and Tradition, brings us to many of the same truths that philosophy teaches us about God—that He exists, that He is infinite, that He is one, that He is personal. But philosophy alone cannot discover that He is a Trinity or that He is incarnate. Those things we know from a whole different point of view, because we begin with God; all religious knowledge begins with God and looks back at the world from His point of view, and we cannot arrive at this point of view by ourselves. Our knowledge must be elevated to this condition, and this begins on earth with our preparation for Heaven.

Let's consider this difference in the context of the greatest question of all: Is Jesus God? The human mind is drawn to two different propositional statements: either Jesus is God, or Jesus is not God. Now, if I were to consider only scientific knowledge, I would have to conclude that one of these propositions was true only by observing Christ. But this is not possible. People in His own time, even those who observed His miracles and knew the prophecies He fulfilled, were uncertain who exactly Christ was. Many believed He was the Messiah, but they couldn't say that they had *scientifically* arrived at such a conclusion in the way we mean that today. This kind of "Christology from below" is popular today because people want to be able to speak the language of science and they question whether theoretical or metaphysical knowledge is really knowledge. But this knowledge cannot replace, or bring us to, true faith.

Indeed, without revelation and without the gift of faith, I would say that we have to conclude, scientifically, that there is no absolute certainty that Jesus is God. Even though all those proofs may be present to my senses, I cannot say *for certain* that they lead to such a grand conclusion. Is faith just the same as opinion, then? If the evidence of unaided reason is inconclusive, do we just fall back on our prejudices? That's the common idea today: "You have your religious opinions and I have mine." Is it just a kind of pious opinion to believe that Jesus is God? Maybe my statement of belief is more based on my emotional need for Him than on any intellectual conclusion: I feel united with Him and so, since I feel He is the Messiah, that is what He means for me.

This isn't the case at all, though. Faith may be unlike any other kind of human knowledge, but *it is real human knowledge*. It is not strictly logical; it is not emotional; it is not just pietistic; it is not just wishful thinking. Faith is the assent of the mind to one proposition: Jesus is God. It is an act of will, but our will to believe does not make it so. Belief is perfected in the will to trust Him in Whom I believe. Faith is the joining of our will to the One who reveals the truth to us. God by His grace enlightens the mind and moves the will to affirm that the one who fulfills the prophecies and does the miracles could not do so unless He were God. Upon this foundation of faith, belief in Jesus as God then is reasonable, and indeed convincing, because Jesus is our avenue to God: It is He, the Son, who teaches us the truth about God and Himself. Yet because the will is always involved in this unique way of knowledge, the Christian continually says with the father who sought a miracle of Christ for his son: "I believe; help my unbelief!" (Mark 9:24). The miracles and prophecies are what theology calls *motives of credibility*. Our faith is not irrational. Still, even those who witness these have no absolute proof.

Faith then allows us to begin to look at the world as God does and to adopt the supernatural attitude of mind and will. "I . . . pray," Jesus says, "that they may all be one; even as thou, Father, art in me, and I in thee, that they also may be in us, so that the world may believe that thou hast sent me" (John 17:20–21). In other words, Jesus wants us to look at the world as He and His Father look at the world, to share in their act of knowing by elevating our minds not to something illogical or absurd, but to the fully integrated, human and divine, potential of our reason. And so the things that are unclear to us become clear to us in Christ.

People who want to reduce the ultimate explanations of this world to material things are, we must say, very primitive. They deny metaphysics and only affirm materialistic explanations like the early Greek philosophers. The early philosophers thought that the whole world would be explained by water. They couldn't get beyond their own noses; they had a true intuition that there was one explanation, but they were exceedingly limited in their manner of discovering what that could be. They did discover after long meditation and contemplation for centuries that material elements could not explain nature fully. In this they discovered God without looking for Him, and so they came to some ideas of metaphysical beings and truths. (Metaphysics means "beyond physics.") But even though they discovered the existence of the cause of the world and some of His attributes, they also discovered they did not know Him by their own power.

True philosophy leads necessarily to the conclusion that all the truths of the world cannot be known or investigated by reason alone. There must be a further science. When Christ came into the world to reveal to us Who God is, a whole level of existence opened to us—a level of existence based on faith that we may now see. That faith must be completed after death in vision in Heaven, which is the direct knowledge of the divine essence without mediation. In this direct experience, through the light of glory, the quest of the will rests and so the soul is fulfilled in joy and peace.

Chapter 4

States of Nature

Grace is necessary first and foremost to arrive at the vision of God. In classical theology, we say that human beings can have three particular kinds of relationship with grace, which we call the states of nature. These states of human nature are still taught today: For example, they form the basis for the first half of the Wednesday Audiences of Pope St. John Paul II known as the "Theology of the Body."

What are these three states of nature? First of all, there is the state of condign nature, also known as the state of original justice or the state of innocence. This was characteristic of Adam before the Original Sin when man was first created in right relationship with God and there was no sin. The second state of human nature is the state of lapsed, or fallen yet redeemed nature. This is the state where we find the human powers we are familiar with, darkened but not extinguished by the sin of Adam and strengthened by the grace of Christ here on earth after the Redemption. The third state is that in which we will be finally complete in Heaven. This is the state of human life after the resurrection of the dead, the state of glorified nature. This is human nature after the manner of Christ's risen body, which shows forth the glory of God and is, truly, human nature fully realized.

What are the characteristics of all these states? Let's begin with the state of original justice. Remember that we have four basic human powers: the body, the emotions, the will, and the intelligence. One can see these powers at work in Genesis 2. The naming of the animals, as we have said, shows that he has an intellect. The commandment concerning the fruit of the forbidden tree, which demonstrates that God is still in charge, shows that he has a will. Man therefore is a composite being, material and spiritual, alone in creation because in naming the animals he finds none like himself. God says it is not good for him to be alone — because God is not alone, but rather three persons who spend all of eternity giving and receiving in love. Vatican II states there are two key characteristics to being a person: Persons must be subjects of love, not objects of use, and persons only realize themselves completely in a sincere gift of self to the other. If this is true of God, it is also true of man.

And so God creates Eve. When Adam sees Eve, who is a person like himself, he gives the first great cry of joy in the history of the human race, and he speaks the first wedding song: "This at last is bone of my bones and flesh of my flesh; she shall be called Woman, because she was taken out of Man" (Gen. 2:23). She reciprocates in silence and returns his love. Then Scripture says: "They were naked and not ashamed" (2:25). This demonstrates complete emotional integrity in virtue, with no possibility of manipulation or competition for power over the other. The body is at peace with the world.

So, in the state of innocence, all four of the powers were in a right order because Adam experienced grace but no sin; man was rightly ordered to God by grace. The experience of God's grace — the experience of knowing as God knows and loving as God loves — created a unity at the very center of what man is, a unity not only in the character but in action. In other words, Adam acted easily and normally as a virtuous person. He experienced infused contemplation continuously, without losing the use of his senses.

(Today, when mystics experience infused contemplation, they enter an ecstasy that deprives them of the usual use of the senses.) Adam's body was constituted to receive this abiding experience of God, so everything he did followed God's directions without delay or struggle. In his will, Adam experienced perfect obedience because of his perfect love for God. He was at peace with God, sharing His inner life. Adam really enjoyed doing the will of God.

I remember teaching a class on this topic, and one of the students asked incredulously if we're really supposed to enjoy being virtuous. Yes! A rightly ordered character is one that doesn't suffer from the weakness of the Original Sin that disposes us against God and toward grumbling and dissatisfaction. So of course you're supposed to enjoy virtuous actions because your human nature is supposed to be a unity, at peace within itself and with God: What you strongly desire in your will should overflow into your emotion so that you enjoy it also. We struggle with this because we don't have this integrity of Adam.

All the same, Adam's body was not a resurrected body. Adam still had to eat to live, and he still had to procreate in order to bring forth human life. But God exercised a marvelous protection over him such that he depended directly upon God's aid for everything he needed. The cause that allowed all this to hang together, like a keystone, was divine grace: Adam had to realize that he had to depend more and more on God's grace in order to preserve his integrity and to share in the divine nature. In other words, he had to lose himself to find himself.

A sign of this original holiness was the fact that Adam and Eve could be married to each other in purity. This was because, in all their conjugal relations, they looked upon themselves in matrimony as an image of the personal union of the Blessed Trinity; therefore, in no sense could they use or manipulate one another. All of God's life is to give. So they looked upon their own lives in marriage as a gift to the other, a gift without extortion. But once the keystone of grace falls through, it is no longer possible for us to use our powers to move toward our ultimate goal. This condition is supernaturally induced: grace, as we will discuss later, is needed to persevere in grace.

There were, then, three kinds of gifts in original justice. The most important kind was the supernatural gift of God's own inner life, the essence of the soul. Second, there were the preternatural gifts. ("*Preter*" means beyond but not above [*super*].) They are: infused knowledge, loving obedience, spontaneity in the passions, and external protection from suffering and death in the body. Finally, there were the natural gifts: the intellect, the will, the passions, and the body. Since man could arrive at his ultimate end, the vision of God, they were all in a marvelous unity of action toward that end.

Grace is human integrity; sin is human destruction. Adam persevered in this integrity for as long as he persevered in his relationship to God's grace. This meant persevering in love—and in its fruit, obedience. But at the temptation of Satan, who was the first disobedient (angelic) person in the history of the world, Adam tried to remain in this condition of original innocence *without* relying on God. In trying to persevere in grace without God's aid, and therefore showing his lack of love for God, he lost grace and entered into the state of Original Sin. He disobeyed the one commandment God had given.

This resulted in the state of fallen nature, into which we are born today. Importantly, this is not a state of total depravity, as Martin Luther would have had it. Man still has good in him. He still has the natural gifts with their final purpose intact. His body, his emotions, his will, and his mind are all good gifts from God, and he can still use them to perform virtuous acts. His intellect is still ordered to truth, his will to loving obedience, his passions to be obedient to reason. But he has lost the supernatural and preternatural gifts, and so he cannot go to Heaven. This is because he has no grace, and so in the state of Original Sin man is not justified, nor can he do meritorious works. He is no longer at peace with God and sharing in divine nature. In the state of Original Sin, our integrity is lost. We cannot act to arrive at the vision of God. The body goes its way and dies; the emotions go their way and desire illicit objects; the will goes its way and tends toward disobedience; the mind goes its way and becomes dulled and darkened.

Why did God allow this to happen? Why did not God just preserve us in the state of innocence? This was because He wished to show us a greater mercy. Man was united to God in nature by grace. Now, by the stupendous miracle of miracles, grace is not only needed so that man may go to Heaven but also has a second effect. Now grace heals from fallen nature, brought to us by a redeemer. In chapter three of Genesis, right after the Original Sin, God promises the Messiah. (See 3:15, where God tells Satan of Eve's descendant, the Messiah, "he shall bruise your head.") God wants to show us that His mercy is even deeper than human weakness and human sin. In other words God allowed Original Sin so that, in His love for us sinners, He might show us how powerful divine mercy really is in reestablishing human justice. In this He is not stymied by human sin from the purpose for which He made man: to show forth His goodness and make us happy with Him in Heaven.

Now the mediation of the Messiah is necessary to experience the grace of redemption. Christ is the new keystone. This also means that our healing hurts. God allows us to experience the loss of grace so that we might share in the Passion of Christ. What for Adam was very easy, for us now is difficult—but we can bear it with Christ's Cross. Virtue was easy for Adam and Eve before Original Sin; not so with us now. We make up what is lacking in the suffering of Christ by applying grace and healing to our own personal lives.

This brings us to the third state of human nature: glorified. This is the state of man truly perfect; grace is finally fulfilled, and we see God face-to-face. Our intellects will be supported not by faith or reason or even infused contemplation, but by the experience of God in Himself. The light of glory is the direct knowledge of the infinite God without mediation. The deepest desire of our will and emotions is fulfilled. This is the completion of the pilgrimage of life, as we arrive at the One we have loved and sought for so long.

Man is then completely unified. The intellect sees God; the will rests in love fulfilled; the passions rejoice; and the body cannot experience suffering and death. This is total sensible joy in the resurrection of the dead and in the presence of God that overflows from our souls into our bodies to shine forth in glory. Indeed, our bodies will be at the instantaneous disposal of our minds, which will themselves be filled with God; all physical limitations will expire. We will look back on the world as God looks at the world, from the point of view of time realized.

This is what real human life is! People today think real human life is the tragedy of sin—no! The weakness of man without grace is a fact, but it is not what it means to be human. The body is meant for the soul, and the soul is meant for God. And only to the extent that we finally enter into the mystery of God can we say that we finally discovered what it means to be truly human. As St. Augustine says, "As the soul is the life of the body, so God is the life of the soul."

Chapter 5

Preparation for Grace

We have established the principle that man is made principally for the vision of God. This requires an elevation of our human powers, that man might realize this purpose. It is essential to remember that human nature is not neutral with respect to God. By the very fact of having an intellect, the spiritual being who is man, created on the horizon of being between time and eternity, must not only have seeing God in the face as his final happiness, but must also be able to progress toward this end in order to experience wholeness and integrity.

This progress requires the Redemption of our state of fallen nature. Once Adam and Eve lost grace, they became alienated first of all from God. Since peace—our reconciliation with God by sharing in His inner life through the Holy Spirit—was absolutely necessary for human integrity, Adam and Eve therefore lost their own integrity with themselves and with the world. In contrast to their original state, which we noted earlier (see Gen. 2:25), they were now naked *and ashamed* (Gen. 3:7). They had lost the perfect control of their reason and bodies and emotions that came with the state of original justice, and they could no longer fully trust one another because they did not trust God.

They became uneasy at their own existence in the world because they were not able to fulfill the purpose of their existence; it felt like creation had shunned them. They hid themselves because they had lost the divine intimacy of grace, and so they then looked on God as a rival. This alienation from God gives rise to an alienation within themselves. They cannot accept life as a gift of love, but they seek to satisfy their longing for meaning by preying on those with whom they originally enjoyed communion of life and love. One of the punishments is directed to both as the will to power: "your desire shall be for your husband and he shall rule over you" (Gen. 3:16). God had questioned each to see how they had come to know they were naked. Each blamed another: the man blamed God, and the woman blamed the serpent.

If this were not enough, creation itself rebelled against man's tillage because it is no longer characterized by disinterested love but by exploitation. Man who was meant to be a steward of creation has now become an exploiter. "Cursed is the ground because of you; in toil shall you eat of it all the days of your life; thorns and thistles it shall bring forth to you; and you shall eat the plants of the field. In the sweat of your face you shall eat bread" (Gen. 3:17–19). The ultimate absurdity then occurs, that a being meant for God returns to dust. Matter seems to triumph over spirit: "You are dust, and to dust you shall return" (Gen. 3:19).

The disorder and domination do not stop with the parents. The children pick it up, and Cain kills Abel. In the Letter to the Hebrews, we read of the faith of Abel: "By faith Abel offered to God a more acceptable sacrifice than Cain, through which he received approval as righteous" (Heb. 11:4). But in trying to recon-nect himself with God, Abel became an occasion of jealousy for his brother, Cain. The riotous and rebellious disunity within the parents' souls was expressed in a riotous and rebellious relation-ship in matrimony, and then it became expressed in a riotous and rebellious relationship of brother to brother.

But it doesn't stop there, either. Look at the history of the Old Testament. Sin slowly enters and permeates the whole world, often in gruesome and perverse ways, until man rebelliously seeks to raise a tower, the Tower of Babel, against God Himself. That is, man seeks to supplant God through technology. In so doing, the very sign of our rationality—our speech—that should be a sign of our reconciliation and union with each other now becomes a sign of our rebelliousness and disunity. The confusion of languages represents and reinforces the confusion of hearts, all caused by the loss of union with God.

Yet God permitted this to bring forth a greater mercy, that in the Redeemer, man should be united to God in Person. The resolution will only finally occur when Jesus, after atoning for all sins on the Cross, sends the Holy Spirit back to us. Babel is reversed at Pentecost. By the sanctifying power of the Holy Spirit, the integrating gift of fellowship with God is now brought back inside human hearts to elevate us again to God's point of view. Only when we adopt God's point of view—only when we are reconciled to Him and call Him our friend and act as a friend would act toward Him—can we become friends with the human race again. Sure, we can pass just laws that direct our exterior conduct and maybe keep people from inciting chaos by punishment, but we can't change them interiorly.

This is the condition in which human beings find themselves as a result of the loss of grace. But God does not leave us here. The cure addresses the sickness right at its source. Remember that there are two principal punishments for the Original Sin: the darkness of the intellect and the malice of the will. Though it's possible for man to understand certain truths, it's very difficult for man to connect those natural things to God as the author of nature simply by his own intelligence. Though fallen man is not totally depraved, he can't love the world as God loves the world, and it is impossible for him to persevere in a right intention toward the things he does love for very long.

Grace Explained

The Original Sin was committed in both the intellect and the will. Thus, God allowed the human race to wander for centuries in this darkness of mind and malice of will principally to teach them their need to rely upon Him, their need for a redeemer. If God had sent the Redeemer immediately after the Original Sin, it would have taught complacency, and so instead He showed us how tragic human life is without Him. Then, at a certain point in time, He chose little by little to begin our cure. He began it with the faith of Abel, a faith that slowly matured over the generations until man began to look to God to direct his life. As an essential part of the process, God established a community in Abraham and then based it on law when He sent Moses to instruct His people that whatever they did here on their earthly pilgrimage affected how they would live after death.

The law revealed on Mount Sinai was a key step in God's preparation of the human race to receive grace again. God chose to enlighten the human mind through His law to show how the nature of the world and human activity, directed by grace, is ordered to Himself.

First, let's consider certain characteristics of law in general. According to St. Thomas Aquinas, a law is "an ordinance of reason for the common good, promulgated by the one who is in charge of the community" (*Summa Theologiae*, I–II, q. 90, art. 4; cf. CCC 1976). The Old Law is an ordinance of reason because it is God revealing His reason to the world. Remember that we are called as human beings to know as God knows, and so in the revelation on Mount Sinai we began again, in a small way, to know the world as God knows it.

And what is the community the divine lawgiver has care of? It is not an earthly state but the community of Israel, the commonwealth of God. The purpose of the kings and the prophets and the priests of Israel was the establishment of the law of God in the hearts of the Israelites. And so through this divine law, human beings were elevated in their intellect to understand again what it was like to act in ordinary things as a person who knew as God knows.

Now, what was the common good of the community of Israel? It was, as it remains for all of us, the vision of God. The juridical precepts existed to orient people again to Heaven. The Temple, after all, was considered to be a representation of the heavenly sanctuary, a shadow of the heavenly Jerusalem (Heb. 8:5). This Temple, of course, would ultimately be the body of Christ, in and through which the perfect worship of God would be carried on, a worship that is truly the result of and productive of reconciliation and peace with God, a worship that makes the participants partakers of divine nature and fulfills them in Heaven by seeing God in the face. Of course, this is Holy Mass.

Finally, the law had to be promulgated. In this case, the law was promulgated by the angels to Moses, while the primary prescriptions were taught by God Himself (see St. Stephen's statement on angels bringing the Old Law in Acts 7:53). It was taught by angels because it was halfway between the natural law known dimly by human beings and the divine New Law taught to us by Christ. The purpose of this law — both the Ten Commandments and the extremely detailed secondary prescriptions in Exodus, Leviticus, and Deuteronomy — was to educate the human mind in what it meant to know as God knows through faith.

The first three Commandments are about worship of God because being reconciled to Him is the cause of human reconciliation, and because participating in divine nature is the only way that man can become truly himself. It's not possible for a person to know the world as God knows the world and to love the world as God loves the world without also loving other human beings as God loves them. And so the last seven Commandments were meant to bring to human minds again what it meant to be a participant in divine nature and to show that the ordinary actions of life have divine repercussions.

And yet we read in 2 Corinthians 3:6 that the Old Law kills. This is because, while in itself the Old Law was good, it could not heal our intellects and our wills, and therefore it was impossible to follow in perfect faithfulness. The law and the ceremonies expanded the Israelites' knowledge of what was right and wrong (and thus their culpability), but it did not communicate grace, nor the presence of the Holy Spirit, to see it through. This doesn't mean the law was valueless, just that it was incomplete. For example, while circumcision could not justify a person, joined with faith in the future Messiah it demonstrated our weakness and the necessity for sacrifice and redemption.

And so, in the Jews' inability to follow what the law commanded, they realized that there was something lacking within themselves. What would be revealed was that this was the presence of the Holy Spirit Himself. This presence could only be restored by a divine figure who would take flesh and would satisfy for the original sin by taking upon Himself its punishment. The faith of Israel, therefore, was a faith that sought to recover this original spirit of being a partaker in the divine nature.

This is shown most beautifully in the elderly Simeon and Anna, who find the One who completes that faith in the Temple, the One who is going to bring back to the world the light and grace they've been waiting for all their lives. As Simeon proclaimed:

> Lord, now lettest thou thy servant depart in peace, according to thy word; for mine eyes have seen thy salvation which thou hast prepared in the presence of all peoples, a light for revelation to the Gentiles, and for glory to thy people Israel. (Luke 2:29–32)

Chapter 6

Old Law, New Law

The Old Law did not perfect man but had as its purpose the preparation of the community of Israel for the Messiah. This is because it could only be lived by grace and neither its rituals (circumcision, the Temple liturgy) or the works it commanded could give grace in themselves. The perfection of the Old Law can only be found in the New Law. This New Law *does* justify because it is not primarily written on stone or paper but on the heart. The New Law—the law of love, the law of the Spirit—is the law that Jesus Christ teaches us (Ezek. 36:26–27; see Matt. 5:17–18).

At the site of the Church of the Holy Sepulchre in Jerusalem, the early Christians believed that they had discovered Calvary, the rock of Golgotha, and the place of Christ's tomb. If you go to that church today and you stand on the rock of Calvary, where tradition holds Jesus was crucified, you can hear rushing water underneath the rock. The early Christians not only maintained that this was the site of the Crucifixion but also that it was the site of Eden. Eden was the source of the natural, life-giving waters of the world, and on Calvary we find the source of the spiritual life-giving waters of the world.

In fact, not only was this place thought to be Eden, but the very place where the Cross stood was thought to be the same place where the tree of the disobedience of Adam stood. When Christ, the New Adam, poured out His blood from that tree to atone for our sins, it rushed down from the Cross, dripped through holes in the rock, and touched the waters of the world, giving them the power to heal from sin by completing the atonement in the sending of the Holy Spirit.

This New Law is expressed by Jesus in the Sermon on the Mount. He ascends a mountain like Moses, but instead of receiving tablets of stone in fire and thunder, He gently instructs us in the Beatitudes. He then applies this to the Old Law by emphasizing the interior perfection of one in love with God.

The essential character of the New Law of Christ is the interior presence and power of the Holy Spirit, who through Baptism enters into the soul. We call this the indwelling of the Holy Spirit. But in order to experience this, one must be elevated by God; one must become a new creation. In the old creation, God brought forth life from nothing; in the new, He brings forth a spiritual life that elevates the soul to Him. It is, in a sense, like creation from nothing because the grace of the Holy Spirit is given without prior merit. It is not that we merit being elevated to this life of the Holy Spirit; it is that God so loves us that He creates this meritorious and justifying character as a result of His loving action. This is in a real sense something new, a true act of creation.

An error that has cropped up through history is the idea that the new, spiritual law means that written, embodied law is obsolete. Remember, of course, that the law of the Old Testament was primarily a written law. On this understanding, there should be no sacraments now that the Spirit has finally come, no physical or external things that lead us to the life of the Holy Spirit. There should be no hierarchy, no priesthood, no religious life. There should be no mediation whatsoever—only the individual soul and the interior life of the Holy Spirit.

This is an extreme distortion that the Church has always rejected. While the New Law of Christ is principally a law of the

Holy Spirit, it is nonetheless true that man comes to experience and understand that law, as in everything else, through sensible things. Thus, if we are to understand what the Holy Spirit wills for us and be disposed to respond to Him, we must be instructed by a written law. That written law includes Scripture, the teaching of the apostles, the teaching of the evangelists, and the Sacred Tradition of the Church, which are expressed in embodied realities like the sacraments. In other words, if we are to live the interior law of the Holy Spirit, we also need, secondarily but no less essentially, the written law.

This does not mean that a person can just obey the letter of the law and be saved in the New Covenant. A person who would coldly obey the prescriptions of the written law but who did not enjoy the divine indwelling of the Holy Spirit would still belong to the times of the Old Testament. By the same token, a person who lived in the times of the Old Testament but obeyed what God commanded through faith in the future Messiah would belong to the times of the New Testament:

> There were ... under the regimen of the Old Covenant, people who possessed the charity and grace of the Holy Spirit and longed above all for the spiritual and eternal promises by which they were associated with the New Law. Conversely, there exist carnal men under the New Covenant, still distanced from the perfection of the New Law: the fear of punishment and certain temporal promises have been necessary, even under the New Covenant, to incite them to virtuous works. In any case, even though the Old Law prescribed charity, it did not give the Holy Spirit, through whom "God's charity has been poured into our hearts" (St. Thomas Aquinas, *Summa Theologiae*, I–II, q. 107, art. 1 ad 2; cf. Rom. 5:5). (CCC 1964)

The New Law, therefore, while primarily spiritual, is also embodied. It has precepts such as liturgy and sacraments, all of which are rooted in Christ and His embodied nature. Christ's flesh is the mediator, the middle ground, the channel through which the grace of the indwelling of the Holy Spirit flows to us. Recall the beautiful priestly prayer of Christ in John 17: "Sanctify them in the truth; thy word is truth" (John 17:17). It is the Holy Spirit sent by Christ on Pentecost who performs this consecration, and the dogmas and the rituals of the Faith are, we could say, extensions that lead us to the Trinity.

Why was the New Law of Christ delayed for so long? First of all, the New Law was not given at the beginning of the world simply because the natural man, i.e., Adam, comes first, followed by the supernatural, i.e., Jesus, the New Adam. "Thus it is written, 'The first man Adam became a living being'; the last Adam became a life-giving spirit" (1 Cor. 15:45). St. Paul doesn't mean that there came first a human being with no spirit, followed by a disembodied human being, like an angel. Rather, he's referring to that interior constitution of body and spirit by which we participate in and ultimately attain the vision of God.

The New Law of Christ, then, was not given as soon as Original Sin was committed because man would not have understood his need for it. Human beings immediately after the Original Sin understood nothing but the materialistic. The early Greek philosophers, as we discussed, figured out that there must be one cause of everything, but the furthest their imaginations could get was, simply, water or other elements. Scientists today have discovered many elements, but in their refusal to admit the need for a spiritual ultimate cause for the universe they remain very primitive. Human beings had to be, in a sense, educated out of this materialistic attitude; they had to discover the world of spirit. The law of Moses was one such tutor. This law progressively prepared human beings so that they could become fit vessels for the Holy Spirit. The Old Law performed a curative function, even though it could not completely heal, the way the New Law can.

The law was given when people had attained such a level of awareness of human life that they understood the necessity of the supernatural order. They knew they needed a kind of healing beyond the bodily. The reason God did not wait longer to send the Messiah was that once attuned to this need for grace, if they had been left without this healing, they might have despaired completely. In the Mediterranean world in the time of Christ, there was on the one hand a growing cynicism toward life itself, and on the other hand a kind of longing to be set free from the limitations of the human condition. In philosophy, Aristotle had come to understand that contemplation of God is what human beings are made for in their souls—and yet there seemed to be no means to arrive at such a thing. So the philosophers who followed Aristotle were filled with the kind of cynical despair about the world.

In the Kingdom of Israel, you'll recall, it seemed that the Jews had finally and completely lost political power and control over their own destinies with the coming of the Romans. At the same time, they had lived many, many generations since receiving the Old Law, but they still had not received consolation from God. They still had not seen the Messiah. The whole purpose of the existence of Israel was to prepare for the Messiah. This is why the cornerstone of the commandments was monotheism. He alone could bring back life to the dry bones of the prophecy of Ezekiel. Yet they had not seen Him. That lack of the interior presence of the Holy Spirit meant that they regularly fell away from even this most fundamental commandment of the Old Law: worshipping the one true God, and Him alone. The baptism of John was a sign of the desire of the people to be cleansed from these wounds, and therefore that the time was right for Christ to come in His flesh to atone for our sin.

The completion of the atonement of Christ consists in His sending the Holy Spirit. So, unlike the Old Law, the New Law is intrinsically justifying because it involves the indwelling of the Spirit. The exterior precepts of liturgy and morality and so on are necessary because of our embodied human nature: they're not necessary because the Holy Spirit needs them but because we need them to receive Him and His gifts, beginning in Baptism, and because they are physically connected to Christ. Christ taught and did works, and as a result teaching and works are a part of the New Law of the Spirit, even though they are not its essence. So in the New Law of Christ we are not justified by works, but works are essential to the living of this law—both in disposing us to it and in executing it. Here is the Letter to the Hebrews quoting the prophet Jeremiah: "This is the covenant that I will make with them after those days, says the Lord: I will put my laws on their hearts, and write them on their minds" (Heb. 10:16).

One last question: Will the New Law of Christ last until the end of time? There will be a fuller revelation of God than that given in the New Law of Christ, but it will not be here on earth. The completion of grace is found in glory. That fuller revelation—the final age of the world—is what will be shown to us when we see God in the face in Heaven and when Christ is revealed finally and fully in His glory in the Second Coming. In this final age there will no longer be sacraments, hierarchies, or a physical need for the Church because we shall know Him directly, "even as we are known" (1 Cor. 13:12).

Chapter 7

Law and Grace

In the Sermon on the Mount, the Lord says, "Think not that I have come to abolish the law and the prophets; I have come not to abolish them but to fulfil them. For truly, I say to you, till heaven and earth pass away, not an iota, not a dot, will pass from the law until all is accomplished" (Matt. 5:17–18). From the very beginning, it is clear that the Old Law is not obsolete; and certainly the Ten Commandments are not. Let's look at how the Sermon is set up.

The evangelist begins by saying that Jesus "went up on the mountain, and … he opened his mouth and taught them" (Matt. 5:1–2). The fact that He ascended a mountain would immediately call to the minds of Matthew's readers the image of Moses going up the mountain. Then, the fact that Jesus Himself opened his mouth and taught would remind them, and should remind us, that Moses was not the direct teacher of the Old Law. Rather, Moses was the mediator by which the Old Law was transmitted from God and His angels. God Himself wrote the Old Law, and Moses presented it to the people, and it was kept in the Ark of the Covenant, which was central to worship in the Temple .

Jesus, then, is the new Moses—but He's a good deal more. He doesn't just present to the people this New Law; He *embodies* the New Law. He is God, and He speaks from the mountain in an embodied and approachable way, whereas the God who gave the Old Law only revealed Himself through terrifying theophanies — manifestations of His presence, such as fire and thunder. Unlike Moses, Jesus sits to proclaim the New Law, which was the posture of authority in the synagogue of His day. The chair of teaching authority is called the *cathedra*, from which our word "cathedral" comes. The New Law issues from His mouth as the Word made flesh.

How, then, does this New Law, spoken directly by the perfect mediator and high priest, relate to the Old Law, which was presented by Moses, who was merely a man? Their purpose, we must say, is the same: to prepare people for the vision of God. That is the end — the fulfillment — of man. The purpose of these laws is to bring back into us the very interior friendship with God, which requires that we share divine life with Him. But they differ in the extent to which they can, in themselves, actualize this goal. The Old Law cures the intellect by teaching; the New Law cures the will by sending grace into the soul.

The Old Law does teach just like the New Law, but the Old Law is like a teacher to children who have not yet interiorized what the true meaning of their conduct is. It has to do with the personal formation of an individual, rather than with making possible loving spontaneous action. The Old Law motivates people mostly by punishment and fear — that is, with an external rod. The New Law, however, since it entails the divine indwelling of the Holy Spirit, is like a teacher for adults, making possible the kind of internal movement of the heart that allows for spontaneous, loving responses to God's will. St. Paul wrote to the Galatians, explaining the maturation made possible by Christ:

> I mean that the heir, as long as he is a child, is no better
> than a slave, though he is the owner of all the estate; but
> he is under guardians and trustees until the date set by the

father. So with us; when we were children, we were slaves to the elemental spirits of the universe. But when the time had fully come, God sent forth his Son, born of woman, born under the law, to redeem those who were under the law, so that we might receive adoption as sons. And because you are sons, God has sent the Spirit of his Son into our hearts, crying, "Abba! Father!" So through God you are no longer a slave but a son, and if a son then an heir. (Gal. 4:1–7)

The Old Law looked forward to the Messiah who would, by His life, death, and Resurrection, bring the possibility of arriving at the vision of God back to the world. The Old Law, which was imperfect in its means, could not bring about that justification apart from relationship to the Messiah. So in the Incarnation of Christ, the Old Law is completed—again, not replaced, but fulfilled—because its rules and rituals were a preparation for His flesh.

The Old Law was oriented to a materialistic people, who were motivated by pleasure and pain. Consider the story of Job, who was deprived of all the material things he had enjoyed, and everyone around him, including his wife, assumed that he would curse God and die. They were still living under the old dispensation and couldn't think outside of it. But Job showed that he had faith in the spiritual promises of the New Law before its time, and so he was justified. He prophesies the resurrection, and his story shows that one can lose all material goods without losing his humanity. After Job survives the trial, though, the values of the Old Law are affirmed because he receives twice the material goods which he lost.

Those material means are fulfilled in Christ, who now gives us better promises. In the New Law of the New Covenant, we have the spiritual promise of Heaven itself. Even though we may suffer and experience punishments, we have the very indwelling presence of the Holy Spirit to support and direct us. The New Law fulfills in Christ the ceremonial precepts of the Old—the rules of the Temple, the washing of all those cups, and all those other things. Christ, in addition, gives us the ability to live better the juridical precepts, and, in His teaching and His works, He also shows us how we are to act.

Does this make the New Law less burdensome than the Old Law? That depends on what we mean by "burdensome." It's certainly easier to remember, since there aren't a great number of prescriptions—613 by the reckoning of rabbis at the time of Christ —that cover every aspect of ceremony and morality. But in its focus on interiority—the spontaneous and joyful movement of the heart toward God born from the right intention of the love of God—the New Law prescribes something much more difficult than simple rule-following. The New Law of Christ demands a right intention, which is nothing less than loving the world as God loves the world. The two great Commandments in Deuteronomy are fulfilled: "You shall love the Lord your God with all your heart, and with all your soul, and with all your mind.... You shall love your neighbor as yourself" (Matt. 22:37–39). We love ourselves, it is important to point out, because we are created by God and receive our existence as a gift from God.

The primary emphasis of the New Law of Christ is on the interior love that is the supernatural, grace-filled presence and power of the Holy Spirit Himself. As we've said, though, this does not mean that there are no exterior works commanded by the New Law of Christ. The first exterior works are those which enable us to have this right intention by first providing and then supporting the life of grace in us—in other words, the seven sacraments. Baptism gives us this life by making us "temples of the Holy Spirit" (CCC 1265); Confirmation further disposes and enables us to defend this life in the face of challenges; the Holy Eucharist supports this life within us by daily food; Confession prepares us to receive the Holy Eucharist worthily and restores this life; Anointing of the Sick disposes us to live this life even in the face of sickness and death; Holy Orders disposes men to be able to bring these sacraments to others; and Matrimony disposes couples to bring this life into the family, the proper field where children are trained to participate in the sacraments.

It is only here, in worship and the sacraments, that the human person discovers his true and full dignity. In Baptism, we become a priest, a prophet, and a king with Christ and so are able to carry on this worship. In the Mass, we conform ourselves to the very worship of Christ on the Cross. In Matrimony, the couple share in both the life of the Holy Trinity, as did Adam and Eve, and in the Cross of Christ by which Christ loves His Church.

So exterior actions are necessary in the New Law of Christ, not just for disposing us to the life of grace, but for living it out. Christ commands both that we avoid sin and that we do good things motivated by the virtue of charity — that is, from a divine point of view. In the New Covenant, this is now a matter of law because the justification of man consists not in what he does but in the divine indwelling of the Spirit that moves him to do it. So we seek to carry out actions that conform to the law of the Holy Spirit and avoid those which corrupt that indwelling.

We avoid adultery, for instance, not just "because the Church says so," but because adultery is against the interior, eternal, self-giving life and love of the Trinity. A person could not profess to have the New Law of Christ and a right intention and also commit such a sin against Him. Avoiding sin may not be sufficient, but it is necessary. Since the New Law of Christ includes the interior presence of the Holy Spirit who inspires us to act, it justifies in itself. Further, the precepts are relatively few in number. One who has the Holy Spirit in his heart and follows Christ in his actions is spiritually free. Such a person is also spiritually mature and thus does not need to have overly specific instructions like children do.

To ensure right intention, the New Law also includes three coun-sels of perfection—poverty, chastity, and obedience—by which we remedy for the three great weaknesses of our nature with respect to growing closer to God: lust of the eyes (poverty), lust of the flesh (chastity), and the pride of life (obedience). These lusts attack right intention and make love less intense. Christ counsels giving up even good things for the sake of something better. Everyone must give up sin, but the counsels recommend having self-control over goods, so we can be sure our intentions are pure. They aren't about Heaven itself but about the means by which we attain Heaven.

Consecrated persons embrace the counsels by vow, and what is a matter of freedom for others becomes an obligation of justice to God in living the virtue of religion. In following these counsels, the religious who take the vows renounce *legitimate* things—pos-sessions, marital intercourse, autonomy—that are not forbidden by the commandments. They are very good but can be the occasion of a great weakness in our character as a result of Original Sin. We've been given grace; we've been called to virtue; we have the Holy Spirit dwelling within us. But even so, the more we love worldly things the more difficult it becomes for us to love spiritual things. And so there can be a great good in denying even legitimate goods in order to liberate ourselves to love and to pursue higher goods.

Those of us who have embraced the counsels by vow—as a Dominican priest, I have done so—encourage others to embrace them on their own, in the ways that suit their life circumstances and their vocations. Vowed religious are supposed to be signs to others that even though they may have and enjoy these things, they should be careful not to love them too much, having as though not having (see 1 Cor. 7:29). In this way we can live out the New Law, which is the law of the Spirit, all the better.

Chapter 8

Grace and Truth

Now that we've laid the foundation of nature and law, we can turn to discussing grace itself. Why do we need grace? First of all, we need grace to know the truth. Grace is a change within us that results from a divine movement of God. We, who are mere creatures, are elevated to God's nature, allowing us to know and to love the way God knows and loves. Now, we don't need God to tell us that the sky is blue; there are many truths we can discern with our senses that don't require His direct intervention. But even so, He does help us. For instance, He does motivate us to study nature, often to discover things we weren't even looking for. After all, God gave us a brain, and He supports the work of this brain in the natural things that we do. Grace isn't necessary for the brain to operate, but it can enlighten us to natural truths that would otherwise elude us.

More importantly, as we have discussed, there are some truths human beings are called to know that we cannot discover by the actions of our own mind. These are truths that require a special quality added to our very being that raises us above our normal manner of knowing, so that we begin to know in a new manner. Principally, the truths that require grace are those that have to do with our knowledge of God in His own intimate life.

For example, to have a personal relationship of friendship with God, it is necessary to know that He is a Trinity. To be prepared for the vision of God, when we shall know even as we are known, we have to get to know the Persons with Whom we will share eternal life. We have to know that Jesus is God made man, which is not evident to our senses. And we have to begin to understand divine providence as God understands it. This special movement of the Holy Spirit is even necessary to know that God exists with firm and resolute certainty. Though reason could discover this, only a few men can do so — and usually with a good deal of error mixed in. But with grace, even a person without any formal education can know this. Aquinas says that because of faith received through grace, such people are greater metaphysicians than Aristotle.

We can do this in part by cooperating with the action of God's grace through growing in the virtues. But even those virtues aren't enough: To really enter into the depths of the hidden life of God, we have to react to the world as if from a kind of divine instinct. Here we can point to the seven sanctifying gifts of the Holy Spirit: knowledge, understanding, wisdom, counsel, piety, fortitude, and fear of the Lord. The action of the Holy Spirit isn't just something exterior to us; it comes from within the very character of our being itself. It is closer to me than I am to myself; it is the capstone of our nature.

So grace is a non-essential help to discovering natural truths, up to and including the truth of the existence of God and certain of His attributes, but it is absolutely essential to understanding and participating in His interior life, which is our highest calling. Even the natural truths acquire an urgent certainty with grace. That's the intellect. What about the will? Is grace necessary to will and to do the good? The answer requires that we make several distinctions.

First of all, just like in the natural truths available to the unaided intellect, there are natural goods available to the unaided will — that is, that are available to us by our own power. These are the natural virtues that we can acquire by our own human love. Is God's grace necessary for us to acquire those? In the state of innocence, remember, grace was not necessary to sustain natural virtues, since Adam lived a completely integrated life, spontaneously responsive to God's will. But in the Original Sin, we fell from that integrated existence, and grace became necessary to heal human nature.

This does not mean that man can't do some good acts without grace. After all, a person can be sick or injured and perform some tasks well, even though he is limited. Some things the person's body could do well, while others it would not be able to perform in accord with its nature. The same is true with human beings after the Original Sin. We can create mighty works of technology, but as to human integrity, this eludes us. So Augustine was of the idea that pagans could still do good works, like building sturdy houses and planting fruitful vineyards. But for the proper virtues of integrity, especially those meritorious of Heaven, only the healing power of grace will do.

Aristotle gave a beautiful and deep picture of human virtue in his *Ethics* but sadly concludes he knows no one like this. Every hero in antiquity has a tragic flaw. Reason could not explain this; we needed to understand that our nature was fallen, and only the Scriptures and sacred Tradition could provide us the solution to this mystery (see CCC 80–82). Grace is needed to heal us so that we can will and do, in an integrated sense, the goods that are proportionate to our nature. Grace is even more needed to be able to look at the world from God's point of view. This means that there can be no truly secular humanism because human beings really can't get their act together, fully, without the aid of grace.

Now, what about loving God above all things? Is grace necessary for this? In the state of innocence, again, it was possible for man to love God above all things without grace because his nature was whole. Everything that exists, even inanimate objects, are called in their way to love God above all things, and Adam was able to do this on his own. There is a certain sense in which an acorn growing into a tree is moved by this to love God above all things. Of course, the acorn does not have a spirit, but still it seeks to return to the unity from which it came. Dante expressed this at the end of his *Divine Comedy* when he wrote that "my desire and will were already moved—like a wheel revolving uniformly—by the Love that moves the sun and all other stars" (Dante, *Paradiso*, 33).

This is the love that is the attraction of each natural being to its Creator, to its source. As God sends forth everything in diversity from Himself, everything seeks to return from diversity to unity by fulfilling its calling. This unity is God. While all creation does this in a limited sense by fulfilling its nature—stars shine; plants grow; antelopes run—only in man can this return be accomplished in its fullness.

After the sin, though, our nature needs to be healed. We who live now require sanctifying grace not only to raise and to elevate us to God's point of view but to support us in doing the things we should do by our own natural capacities in their most perfect sense. What about following the commandments of God? Do we need His help for that? The fourth-century monk and heretic Pelagius taught that man, by his own strength, could observe all the commandments in every way whatsoever. This is the primordial heresy about grace. Pelagius was an ascetical person who practiced great penances, and he looked upon those penances—that is, his works—as his justification. The Church rightly condemned this teaching, which corrupted Her doctrine of penance and good works by claiming that by our actions we can, somehow, force God to love us or elevate our own nature to Heaven. In a sense, we could boast of our works before God and demand a kind of justice from Him. Augustine says clearly, "Before God there is no boasting."

When it comes to obeying the commandments, let us again distinguish between the state of innocence and the state of fallen nature. In the state of innocence, man could do the substance of the works called for by God without grace — *but even in this state* he needed grace to do these works from a right intention, which was necessary if he were to obey the Commandments correctly. After Original Sin, we are even more dependent on Him: We can't even perform the substance of the works without grace. We need the change effected in us by grace in order to heal us and therefore to enable us to do what we're supposed to do, as well as to do it from the right motive.

That right motive can only be brought to us by the divine fire that Christ brought to the earth. "I came to cast fire upon the earth; and would that it were already kindled!" (Luke 12:49). This is not an exterior fire but the fire of charity, the fire of the Holy Spirit, the fire that comes to and from a person who understands and loves God's heavenly point of view in his very soul.

When, by grace, we allow God to move us in His way, then step by step we approach that homesickness for Heaven described by the saints and mystics. We grow in that desire to see God in the face, which led Teresa of Avila to say, "I'm dying because I don't die." Love born of grace in faith does not still our longing but sets it aflame even more. One wants to see the Beloved, directly.

It is a paradox of the mystics that the more works they do, and the more they experience God's grace in them, they seem to grow in both happiness and unhappiness. They are more fully alive than ever, and yet emotionally they experience a kind of death because they want only to be with their Beloved. St. Paul wrote to the Philippians, "My desire is to depart and be with Christ, for that is far better. But to remain in the flesh is more necessary on your account" (Phil. 1:23–24). Paul wanted to be with God, but God wanted him to spread His message of divine life to the people of this world so that they, in their ordinary lives, might come to desire Heaven, as well.

How rich our lives are, that we have been called by charity to enter into the point of view of divinity itself, and that in grace we have a form added to our nature that elevates our nature to that point of view. It does not corrupt or destroy or change our nature but fulfills it, bringing our mortality to His infinity. It allows us to begin, in the ordinary things of life, to look at the world from the point of view of the Holy Spirit.

The great philosophers of the Enlightenment looked upon this truth as somehow alienating man from his natural reason. For them, religion was at best an emotional substitute for reason. What the Church teaches is that though we respect reason and science in their natural realms, no amount of scientific progress can solve the mystery of man, the mystery of death, or the mystery of human evil. Real human science leads to the conclusion that a further knowledge and love is necessary. This is divine intimacy and is caused only by grace.

We cannot in any sense elevate ourselves to eternal life without God's divine aid. Grace is absolutely necessary for this, and it is this in which human perfection consists. The restlessness of man can only be stilled by the added quality, this divine instinct, of grace.

Chapter 9

Preparation and Perseverance

Having discussed how grace is necessary to do supernatural goods, to perfect us in the virtues, and to merit eternal life, the question now arises: Do we need grace also to prepare us to receive this divine movement? Some theologians have thought that we can prepare ourselves for grace by our own power, but this has come to be known as the heresy of semi-Pelagianism — a halfway attempt to knock God out of the picture that puts us on the path to Pelagius's more serious error. But if we look at grace as the force that moves us to act rightly, then we must say that, yes, our wills certainly have to be prepared by this force.

In St. John's Gospel, we read a definitive statement from Jesus: "No one can come to me unless the Father who sent me draws him" (John 6:44). So while our ongoing conversion to Christ does involve our free wills — God never acts in anything against its nature — the initial inspiration in our will is a movement of the Holy Spirit — supporting us, drawing us, preparing us.

Now, we can also use our free will to reject this preparation. Consider Augustine, who for many years accepted Christianity as true in an abstract, intellectual way, before finally choosing to be baptized. He struggled to fully accept things that he could not completely demonstrate to himself, so despite his philosophical convictions he could not bring himself to say he was a Christian.

Later, he always attributed his final and full conversion to the prayers of his mother, St. Monica, who besought Heaven until, around the age of thirty-five, he opened himself to and accepted God's preparation.

And so we need grace to be able to receive grace. The first movement always belongs to God. As you know, however, it's very important to make distinctions. So here let us distinguish between the two kinds of grace that God offers to us. The grace of elevation to partake of the divine nature, which we have been discussing in the previous chapters, is, again, called "sanctifying grace." The grace of preparation is different: we call it, as we first noted in chapter one, "actual grace." Whereas sanctifying grace is always, by definition, an internal quality within the soul itself, God's actual grace can occur in anything that we experience—either exteriorly or interiorly—that disposes us to the movement of the divine fire which is the Holy Spirit.

It follows from this that we need God's grace to rise from original and actual sin in our present state. This means more than just ceasing to perform the sinful action. There are three aspects to the condition of sin, the first being the "stain"—the interior corruption that endures after the fact. Sin darkens our ability to respond to the enlightenment of God and so to merit Heaven, and it is not possible, by our own power, to restore our access to that divine light. Grace is absolutely necessary because by grace God enters and enlightens us again, supplying for our defect with His divine power.

The second characteristic of the condition of sin is the corruption of the will. In every mortal sin, the natural tendency of our wills toward good is corrupted, such that we cannot turn it back to pursue that good. We need grace to open that door again. Lastly, there is the punishment due to sin: In the case of mortal sin, this is the loss of grace and thus the ability to go to Heaven. Is it possible for us to make up for that punishment without grace?

Absolutely not: God's interior movement is necessary to resolve for the debt of punishment that each of us experiences as a result of sin, by seeking repentance and confession. In all these ways, then, it is necessary for God to free us from sin by the interior change of sanctifying grace—healing, aiding, and supporting us in turning from sin back to Him. "Restore us to thyself, O Lord, that we may be restored!" (Lam. 5:22). Actual grace turns us and opens us, by repentance and confession, to the forgiveness of sins.

What about avoiding sin in the first place—do we need grace for that? Here we have to return to our distinction between the state of innocence and the state of fallen nature. In the state of innocence, due to Adam's perfect integrity he was able to avoid all sins, both mortal and venial, without the aid of the internal change of sanctifying grace. However, Adam still required the support of actual grace to remain in God's friendship, a grace he failed to cooperate with in the first sin. In our state of fallen nature, however, it is impossible for us to avoid sin without the qualitative internal change in our being effected by sanctifying grace. As we said, our fallen state is not totally depraved, so we can do some good and avoid some sin on our own. But a complete detachment from sin requires God's transformative power in our souls to heal us from the defects of our nature.

This leads us to conclude that, with the help of sanctifying grace, we *can*, in fact, avoid all mortal sins. There is a dangerous minimalism in some areas of the Church today that insists or implies that, even with God's help, some mortal sins—especially sexual sins—are just unavoidable. They say that the idea of perfect detachment from such sins is unrealistic or idealistic. This is simply not true. If God enters into us and supports us with His divine life, it should be eminently possible for us to avoid all mortal sins, including sexual sins.

That being said, it is certainly true that despite being saved through the reception of sanctifying grace in Baptism, we still suffer from the weakness of the Original Sin, which means that we often have inordinate movements toward the passions in our character. People go to Confession in anguish because they feel that even though they have not committed a particular sin, they have had an interior movement that has enticed them. First of all, it is no sin simply to be tempted. One must will the thing to which one is tempted. Second of all, even if we cooperate in some way, interiorly or exteriorly, with some sinful inclination, we should remember that we cannot avoid all venial sins. The only person who never committed a venial sin was the Blessed Virgin Mary. Everyone else has at least one.

However, grace does allow us, even in our fallen condition, to avoid all mortal sins and to avoid as many venial sins as is possible. In other words, grace is absolutely necessary for people to realize their full potential as human beings. This extends to persevering in the condition of grace once we have been elevated. In the eighteenth century, the Jansenists taught that once Adam received the grace by which he was elevated to be a partaker of God's nature, he no longer needed to rely on God's assistance. They attributed the fall of Adam to his own power — this part was correct — but then they attributed Adam and Eve's own rising again to new life to their own power. Before the sin, man, who was created in grace, could persevere, they thought, in such a supernatural state without the further aid of God continuing to enlighten his mind and strengthen his will.

But God does not give us His love to free us to ignore Him. God does not elevate us to be like Him and then no longer expect us to depend upon Him. The loving relationship we have with God demands that in all the things we experience in life, even when He feels far from us in our thoughts and emotions, we realize that He is, in fact, more intimate to us than we are to our very selves and so is supporting us every step of the way. A person who experienced the love of God in transforming union would not think he could persevere in such a state without the Beloved, but he would instead know that he must continuously rely on the Beloved each day to endure in such a state until death. This is both because of the supernatural life introduced into the soul by grace and the desire to avoid giving into moral weakness and sin. Each day even the holy ones on earth must pray: "Lead us not into temptation, but deliver us from evil."

First of all, God has to assist everything that exists in order for it to continue in existence. If God forgot a single fly, it would cease to exist, passing into nothingness. If God's assistance is needed to support our very existence in this world, it is certainly needed even more so to support our supernatural elevation. Therefore, we are called to a life of continuous prayer—continuous willing and knowing as God wills and knows, continuous acts of faith, continuous acts of charity—so we can experience the depth and power of God. The very nature of the act which caused Original Sin was that Adam and Eve made a decision about the commandments without relying on the Beloved for enlightenment and support.

Those who write about the mystical life maintain that one of the reasons there are so few people who experience this kind of intense contemplation is that the instant God begins to draw us beyond ourselves to His way of doing things, we find it difficult to follow by surrendering control to Him. We no longer look and ask for His assistance. "Ask, and it will be given you; seek, and you will find; knock, and it will be opened to you" (Matt. 7:7). As soon as our emotional high in a relationship of prayer and grace starts to diminish, as soon as we fail to get what we want when we want it, we stop asking, seeking, knocking. Right when we have the opportunity to grow even more, we stop relying on divine aid. Even the saints in Heaven, who already see God in the face, are not thereby freed from the necessity of God's assistance: They still rely on Him, even in His presence. If this is true of them, then of course it is even more true of us.

It is common to experience deep emotional joy after an intense conversion to grace. This is a kind of spiritual honeymoon. But that feeling does not last, just as the post-wedding honeymoon does not last. In marriage, one must face the day when the passionate feelings fade and one must get down to the business of losing one's ego to and for another. It is the same in the spiritual life of grace. Life can be tough and burdensome, and it becomes difficult to see and to recognize the face of God. It would be a mistake to base one's prayer life on the *feeling* of closeness with God, a psychological condition that is, at most, a reflection of the real thing. It's like a husband or wife trying to reproduce the emotions of the honeymoon decade after decade: It won't work, and the couple can become disappointed. We have to trust our *objective* relationship with God and always rely on that—which is how we strengthen it.

This all is not to denigrate emotions. Emotions can be very good: God gave them to us, and they are one of the ways we experience Him. But they are not the measure of progress in grace. Sometimes, in fact, it may be just the opposite. A feeling of dryness or even spiritual darkness can be a sign of maturity in the life of grace, as we grow accustomed to relying on God and His ways, instead of the world and our own feelings.

This is important because it is essential to our sanctification and salvation that we continue to persevere in grace. Some Protestant sects preach a "once saved, forever saved" doctrine that says that it is impossible to fall away once one has given oneself to Christ. This is because they interpret grace not as a quality but as a feeling of confidence that Christ will save them no matter what they do. This is very dangerous: The true teaching of the Church is that one is never finally confirmed in grace in this life. Even Adam, in his marvelous integrity, was not fully confirmed in grace. With the exception of the Blessed Virgin, who was confirmed in grace at the Annunciation when she conceived Jesus in her body by the action of the Holy Spirit, this only happens when we see God in the face in Heaven. We all need to pray for the grace of perseverance. No one can presume that because he has been called, he will therefore be chosen (see Matt. 22:14).

Grace is a love affair with the Beloved in which we are elevated to a condition beyond what we can achieve, or imagine, on our own. To say that we do not need God's aid anymore to persevere in this condition of love is to disregard the Beloved just as the relationship is getting started. This was the sin of Adam — to try to dispose of the supernatural as he wished. Remember, as Jesus teaches, "No one can come to me unless the Father who sent me draws him" (John 6:44).

Chapter 10

Kinds of Grace

Now that we have discussed the necessity of grace, we can turn to the nature and kinds of grace, and thus examine the deepest and most beautiful of mysteries: what grace is. By grace the human soul is elevated to participate in the life of the Trinity. How is it that we remain human and yet in some sense are elevated to the very being of God?

As usual, understanding the answer will require definitions and distinctions, starting with a few terms from philosophy, specifically the field of metaphysics: substances and accidents. A substance is a being that exists in its own right. To be clear, this is very different from a chemical substance, which is a material with consistent properties and chemical composition, such as water or gold, that can be combined with other substances to make an individual object or being, such as a cactus or a lizard. Rather, it is these complete, self-contained wholes—a plant, an animal, a rock, a human—that are substances in the metaphysical sense. Substances are only found in natural beings, not ones created by human artifice. Artificial things—chairs, tables, houses—are accidental combinations of substances, including types of wood and other materials.

An accident, on the other hand, does not exist in its own right; it is a kind of being that must exist within another, complete being. The color pink, for example, does not exist apart from a pink cloth. The qualities of hardness or softness do not exist outside of the physical reality of diamonds or stuffed animals, for instance. "Place" is a kind of accident: I do not transform into a different kind of being (a different substance) when I walk from the kitchen into the living room.

Accidental qualities can also include moral and spiritual realities. When I become virtuous, I don't destroy myself or change myself into something besides a man; I simply become a better man. Finally, health is an example of an accidental quality applied to the body as a whole: health is the manner in which a body exists as complete and effective and strong, while sickness is the manner in which a body exists as ineffective and weak. The body, again, remains the same in its substance, but it has a different (accidental) qualitative way of existing.

Grace, then, is health of the soul. By grace, the human soul is qualitatively raised to enjoy God's own life. Grace, therefore, while it doesn't transform the person into a different *substance*, is still a true interior change. It is *not* just God overlooking the sickness of the soul, with the soul remaining in exactly the same condition as it was before the reception of grace. Martin Luther, who taught that man was totally depraved by nature, said that reconciliation with God simply involved God overlooking our depravity. This is called "forensic justification," and it basically means, if we think of a courtroom setting, that the judge (God) lets me off the hook, but I remain a completely guilty murderer.

The Lutheran position is characterized by saying that human nature in grace is "a lump of dung covered by snow." We, the dung, were never changed. Justification, on this understanding, is merely the overlooking of sin and does not actually change human nature, except in a psychological sense. So even in the state of grace, man remains totally depraved. This is how the false doctrine of "once saved, always saved" comes about.

The Catholic Church has always taught that grace involves a true interior change which is *both* the forgiveness of sins *and* something more: the divine indwelling of the Holy Spirit. Justification, then, is both the forgiveness of sins and the indwelling of the Spirit. This is transformative and restorative, not just a papering-over of evil. Grace is a result of God's love, and He does not just leave us as we are. In human love, we respond to a lovable quality we already find in a person. This is not true of God's love, which does not respond to already-existing qualities in things but rather brings those qualities into being. After all, God's love brings forth our being to begin with; everything that exists does so because God loves it into existence.

And so, for reasoning beings like us, God gives a further quality of His love. When God remits our sins, He does so by sending the Holy Spirit to dwell in our souls to qualitatively raise them so that we can have a loving conversation with Him in the ordinary course of our lives. Sanctifying grace, then, is a disposition or quality of being—a true interior change—by which we become a new creation and in which we partake of the divine nature itself. Man raised up by grace is called a new creation because as God created something from nothing in the first creation, He introduces something brand-new—grace—into our souls without prior merit. Man becomes a new creation not as something different than a being having a human soul and body, but as a being able to act perfectly to fulfill the purpose of that soul's creation. The term *habit* is a good one for this because it simply means a new kind of existing with new possibility of acting: to know as God knows and love as God loves. We do not become God, but we act as He does.

Therefore, grace does more than change our abilities; it changes our very selves, elevating them to new possibilities, because it elevates the soul itself to a divine kind of existence. Just as health enables the body to be its very best, so grace enables the soul to be its very best, as it was made to be. There can be no human soul at its best that does not have the intimate indwelling of the Father, the Son, and the Holy Spirit. That's what we are called to; that's what our hearts are restless for. Grace, then, enters into not just our powers—the emotions, the intellect, and the will—but into the very center of our souls themselves. It is this, then, that influences how we think, how we love, how we feel, and what we do.

It is like the string of a violin, which exists in its own right, but then the violinist comes along and imparts to it a movement that is beyond its independent capacity. Thus the musician imparts a new quality of existing by pulling the bow over it and creating friction (a kind of suffering, perhaps) and vibration, giving the string the ability to produce a beautiful sound. God by grace comes to our soul and gives that soul the ability to produce true human beauty, which is a beauty that reflects and is influenced by God. And so we can also say that grace is the beauty of the soul. The psalmist says, "Thou dost cause ... oil to make his face shine" (Ps. 114:14–15).

Not only that, but this exciting doctrine also entails a power of divine love that goes beyond creation: "It is the opinion of St. Augustine that 'the justification of the wicked is a greater work than the creation of heaven and earth,' because 'heaven and earth will pass away but the salvation and justification of the elect ... will not pass away'" (CCC 1994).

One could then define sanctifying grace like this: "an habitual gift, a stable and supernatural disposition that perfects the soul itself to enable it to live with God, to act by his love" (CCC 2000). This is to be distinguished from actual grace which, as we've noted earlier, is not a qualitative change to the soul but merely divine aid. Actual graces "refer to God's interventions, whether at the beginning of conversion or in the course of sanctification" (CCC 2000). So by actual grace God enlightens the mind and strengthens the will to know and love in a divine way.

These two types of graces are further distinguished from a third kind: charismatic grace. The Church traditionally teaches that the love of God is experienced in two ways, distinguished in chapters 12 and 13 of 1 Corinthians. In chapter 12, St. Paul talks about God's giving people the ability to perform actions that lead other people to prepare themselves for grace; these are sometimes called "charismatic graces," such as healing, miracles, prophecy, etc., because of the charisms they inspire in us (see 1 Cor. 12:8–10). We also believe that the ability to confect the sacraments is a kind of charism given to priests through the Church by the Sacrament of Holy Orders. The ability of the pope to speak infallibly on matters of faith and morals is also a charismatic grace. These are graces that are freely given by God for the sake of leading other people to salvation. A priest who preaches a beautiful sermon is an instrument by which others come to grace; a person who speaks the truth confidently and prophetically is an instrument by which others come to grace; and so on.

Does this mean that the person who exercises these charismatic graces must himself be holy? Of course it would be best if he were, but these graces are freely given by God for the sanctification of others and are not contingent on the sanctity of His instruments. (This is a way these graces differ from sanctifying grace, which makes us pleasing to Him.) So a person could possibly speak in tongues, for instance, while leading a wicked life. St. Augustine says that when Caiaphas, as the high priest of Israel, said it was expedient for one man — Jesus — to die for the people (see John 11:50 and 18:14), he was truly exercising the gift of prophecy, but not for his own holiness. It was wicked for him to say this even though God was using his words to teach truth, because God is never stymied by the weakness of his instruments. It is therefore possible for a person to experience a charismatic grace of the Holy Spirit and not themselves be pleasing to God.

Grace Explained

Then, at the end of that chapter of 1 Corinthians, St. Paul says, "I will show you a still more excellent way" (1 Cor. 12:31). The beginning of the next chapter is one of the most famous in all of Scripture:

> If I speak in the tongues of men and of angels, but have not love, I am a noisy gong or a clanging cymbal. And if I have prophetic powers, and understand all mysteries and all knowledge, and if I have all faith, so as to remove mountains, but have not love, I am nothing. If I give away all I have, and if I deliver my body to be burned, but have not love, I gain nothing. (1 Cor. 13:1–3)

Love here ("charity" in other translations) refers to the effect of the grace when the Holy Spirit enters our souls and elevates us to this divine life. In other words, Paul is referring to sanctifying grace, which is not only freely given and without prior merit, but also makes the soul like unto God. That's why Paul says that "love is patient and kind; love is not jealous or boastful; it is not arrogant or rude" (13:4–5). By this grace, and not by charisms alone, we come to know the world as God knows the world, and to love the world as God loves the world.

One must beware of thinking that one is holy because of the spiritual gifts one has been given. A preacher or a teacher has to beware of thinking that, because he can explain the truth to people and move them to conversion, he himself is certainly holy. He must practice what he preaches in his own life, entering into deep prayer; he is not freed from the obligation to do that because he is pastorally successful. Religion is not about success; it is about giving and receiving the love of God and neighbor.

One can thus distinguish moments in the reception of grace: The same interior presence of the Holy Trinity has two results. The first is that grace moves us, and we allow ourselves to be moved by it; this is the instance of the first conversion, the foundation of further grace. I merit nothing from this, so we must say that if people look upon their works as meriting grace, they are mistaken. Catholicism has never taught that you can merit grace, which is given by God freely. He wills it to anyone who is disposed to it. This effect of sanctifying grace is called justifying, or operating grace, because by it God performs His own supernatural actions.

To this grace corresponds another kind, cooperating grace, by which God entices — but does not force — our free will. God never acts in a thing against its nature, and it is in the nature of human beings that we act by our free will. To be clear, free will does not *cause* our justification, but we may allow our wills to be moved by the divine indwelling that is our justification. In other words, in order for us to progress toward Heaven, we have to choose to listen to and to work with God's divine movement within us. We have to move all our powers to cooperate with this qualitative change in the soul. I come to desire Heaven more the more I adhere to God. This enjoyment, then, is further demonstrated by the choices I make in my own moral life.

Keep in mind these two truths: That God creates us without us, which is an act and fruit of divine love; but He will not save us without us. He entices our free will and divinizes our souls through prayer, penance, and good works, even though these do not *merit* the free gift of grace. What these acts do merit, however, is our reward for our whole life: the vision of God in Heaven. That is, we do not merit justification, but rather that which flows from justification, which is Heaven. It is a true reward given to us because God has elevated us and supports us in this cooperating grace to pursue it.

By grace each of us has the chance to have Heaven begin here on earth for us. Each of us begins to get to know the Trinity, to become familiar with God, and to be able to carry on a conversation with Him throughout our lives — a loving conversation that influences our works and increases the fire of our love. The more we love God on earth, the deeper will our vision of Him in Heaven be. We must therefore continuously rely on and prepare ourselves to partake of that divine nature.

Chapter 11

Mediators of Grace

We know that God alone can introduce grace into us because He is the only one who possesses infinite truth and love in His very being. But an objection may arise: If God alone is the cause of grace, do we need any human mediators? This objection is often voiced regarding sacramental Confession to a priest in the Church. People will say that they feel their sins are forgiven in private prayer: therefore, they don't need any priest or any church to get involved.

The difficulty with that way of looking at things, however, is that it suggests that divinity comes to us in a completely spiritual, disembodied way that is basically inhuman. The truth is that God uses physical intermediaries—not because *He* needs them to bring grace to us, but because *we* need them; because they are the most human ways possible to bring His divine action to us. We are not angels who have no bodies, and so the physical body is an important part of our experience of truth and love.

Plato, for his part, sought to devalue the physical once he discovered the spiritual. But Aristotle corrected him from the wisdom of everyday experience. The human mind is a blank slate when a person is conceived, and sense knowledge and love are necessary components in experiencing spiritual knowledge and love. The body is in no sense evil but rather is a good created by God, who does not make any mistakes.

Grace Explained

Of course the physical body of Christ is the most perfect instrument, the most perfect mediator, the most perfect means that God has used to reveal Himself to us and to bring His action to us. Christ's human nature, joined to the second Person of the Trinity, has power in itself to bring the action of divine grace to humanity. This Person is the Word, Who in His human nature has a human body, a human soul, and human emotions. Through these, Christ becomes the instrument by which God, Who alone is the cause of grace, brings that grace to us.

A person who says that he doesn't need anything physical between himself and God — any church, priest, etc. — may as well say that he also does not need the physical nature of Christ. That human nature of Christ extends through time and space into and through the sacraments and hierarchy of the Church. Traditionally, we say that the human nature of Christ is like the hand joined to the body, an integrated part of God's action, while the sacraments are separated instruments, which accomplish the will of the Master but are not strictly part of Him — but rather like a craftsman's hammer. Therefore we say that the sacraments do not cause grace *by* themselves but rather *in* themselves, inasmuch as they channel the power of Christ's physical humanity, which is the true cause of grace because it is united to the primary source of divine power. This is the Person of the Word.

While God is all-powerful, grace does not work like magic. We must be prepared for and disposed to His divine action — a preparation, as we have said, that He Himself initiates through grace. God never acts in anything or anyone against the nature which He has given to it or him, and our nature is to have free will. Therefore, for human beings to be disposed to receive Him, our free will cannot have placed a block in His way. Just as a piece of wood has to be prepared by heat to burst into flame, so the human will has to at least be open to receiving the movement of God in sanctifying grace.

This does not mean that God is *limited* by our free will; God is not limited by what He finds in us. In adults, the preparation for the sanctifying grace of the sacraments of initiation is called catechesis, and this does require our free will. But babies who are baptized have not yet developed their wills, and yet they receive grace because they put no obstacle in the way of it. When babies grow older and their free will begins to operate, though, they need to receive catechesis to understand how to conform their wills to Christ, so that grace can operate most fruitfully.

That covers sanctifying grace, but is there preparation needed for actual grace? Not at all: It is distinctive to this kind of grace that it comes seemingly out of nowhere. Sometimes, through actual grace, God can act upon the soul to prepare it instantaneously for sanctifying grace: This we can see in the story of the conversion of St. Paul. But that is not the way it usually works. Look at St. Augustine, who was around thirty-five years old before he finally accepted sanctifying grace, after many years of resisting the movement of God within Him in actual grace. But once he did accept it, the result was a magnificent movement of God that beautified his soul wholly and completely.

As a priest, I have seen this happen first-hand. One night, as I was locking up my church, a woman was riding her bicycle, stopped, and told me that she was married to a non-practicing divorced Catholic and had herself never been baptized, but she was very curious about the Catholic Faith. She asked if she could take some instruction from me, so that's what we did. Around the fourth class, which was about grace, she spontaneously shouted, "Oh Father, I want grace!" Just a little bit of catechesis, just a little bit of time, was all the preparation for grace she needed to realize that conviction. She had to patiently wait for two years for her husband's first marriage to be annulled by Rome, but her conviction was so strong that she persevered. Every time those of us who are baptized and confirmed Catholics fall away in mortal sin, then go to Confession, that is a statement that we want grace—that we are responding to God's preparation to accept the divine indwelling once again.

Now, God is not *necessitated* to give grace to someone who has prepared himself. That would go against His perfect freedom. But it is also in His nature to be perfectly and completely self-giving. So He will supply what we need if we are ready for it, but not because we force His hand. He does it because He has promised it, and He always fulfills His promises.

This also means that as our disposition to grace becomes stronger, we can *grow* in grace. It's not all or nothing, as in the "forensic justification" taught by Martin Luther. Luther's concept of "overlooking" or "covering over" our sinfulness also led to two more errors: that we could know for certain if we had grace, and that receiving grace was a permanent guarantee of salvation. In other words, it was thought, and still is by many Protestants today, that once you accepted Jesus it was impossible for you to fall away. This mistakenly makes initial sanctifying grace the same as the grace of final perseverance.

There is nothing wrong with having a psychological confidence in God, but neither is that the *basis* for our relationship with Him, nor is it a *sure sign* of that relationship. The objective reality of the divine indwelling is sharing a common life with the Trinity, but that will not always feel perfect—just like a husband and wife will not always feel perfectly in love. Furthermore, any relationship takes time—preparation, right disposition, and so on—to develop. Being a child of God means really and truly sharing in God's life, and this kind of relationship requires preparation and ongoing effort. When Teresa of Avila wrote the *Interior Castle*, she did not waste time on methods and other procedures. She stated that living the Christian life—rooting our everyday faults and growing in everyday virtues—was the proper preparation for growth in prayer.

Grace is a supernatural state, so unless God directly enlightens us, we cannot know for sure if we are in the state of grace, because this would require perfect access to the interior life of God that is not possible in this world. Remember the parable of the wheat and the tares, where the master says, "Let both grow together until the harvest" (Matt. 13:30). Only in God's time and in God's wisdom will we truly know who is in His friendship and who is not. As St. Paul wrote, "Work out your own salvation with fear and trembling" (Phil. 2:12).

This doesn't mean we should live as if we can have no inkling of our state, as if our salvation is random or arbitrary. We may not have mathematical certitude that we have grace, and certainly not that we will persevere in grace in the future, but we can have a reasonable certainty based on all the signs that Christ has told us about a person who loves Him. If we are not conscious of being in mortal sin, that is a very good sign that we are not, in fact, in a state of mortal sin. If we are living out the Commandments and the Beatitudes, worshipping Him, and loving Him in the everyday course of our lives, those, too, are very good signs that the grace of God is acting within us. As the Lord tells St. Paul, "My grace is sufficient for you" (2 Cor. 12:9).

If a Catholic is asked if he is saved, his response should be that of St. Joan of Arc, which is referred to in the *Catechism of the Catholic Church*. "A pleasing illustration of this attitude is found in the reply of St. Joan of Arc to a question posed as a trap by her ecclesiastical judges: 'Asked if she knew that she was in God's grace, she replied: "If I am not, may it please God to put me in it; if I am, may it please God to keep me there"'" (CCC 2005).

As for growing in grace, we should first note that, in its sanctifying character, God offers the same divine life to all. God does not offer a higher-proof sanctifying grace to some than to others. But, as any teacher knows, you can offer the same enlightenment to a group of people, and some will take it in more effectively than others. I have had the experience of quizzing students at the end of a semester and being told the exact opposite of what I had taught. This is because we receive enlightenment, either of the mind or of the spirit, not according to the mode of the giver but according to the mode of the receiver.

In the matter of grace, that just means that we are all not prepared to receive God's gifts in the same way. The extent of our preparation, which is itself a reflection of our love for God, can determine how much we experience the influence of grace—and that preparation and experience can grow over time. In the prophecy of Malachi we read, "For he is like a refiner's fire and like fullers' soap; he will sit as a refiner and purifier of silver, and he will purify the sons of Levi and refine them like gold and silver, till they present right offerings to the Lord" (Mal. 3:2–3). A refiner takes the metal and puts it in a crucible, and then he applies incredible heat and violent agitation. In this process, the impurities become separated from the metal and can be scraped away. If you were to ask the refiner how he knows that the time has come when the metal can be fashioned into a beautiful vessel, he will say, "When I can look inside the crucible and in the metal see my own image reflected." Jesus wants to see His reflection in the mirror of our souls.

The preparation of man to receive the action of God is the same: the trials of life, and the good things of life, stir us up, helping us to realize that our end is not here, that our conversation should be in Heaven, and that the value of a human person does not consist in what he does but in what he is. In other words, they help us to prepare ourselves to become more receptive to the action of God. God alone is the cause of grace, but by His actual grace He stimulates us and prepares us so that when He looks into our souls, He may see the truth and goodness with which He feels at home.

Chapter 12

Justification

In these final two chapters, we will consider the results, or effects, of two kinds of grace: operating grace (justification) and cooperating grace (merit). Let's begin by returning to a definition of operating grace: the initial movement of God within us that moves our free will. That free will, as we have said, has to be capable of being moved (that is, we cannot have blocked it from being moved), but we only participate in this movement in the sense that we receive it. This is the initial movement of grace, and it is what makes our souls to be right in God's eyes. Since our souls are spiritual, it is necessary that in order for them to be right, we must in some sense share life with God.

It is a fundamental point of this book that both angels and human beings have as their final purpose seeing God in the face, knowing Him directly, by the light of glory, and that humans have to be prepared for this purpose while on earth by our free choices. But we have to experience the true life of God within us if our free choices are to conform to the way He knows and loves. It is in this first result of grace that man, in his soul, becomes righteous and just: the usual term for this is "justification," by which we truly become a child of God.

Justification in the theological sense is righteousness. It does not refer to the virtue of justice, which is in the will and regards giving to each what he is due. It rather refers to a right relationship in acting among the intellect, the will, and the passions, all moved in integrity by God. The disorder in these powers is traditionally known as concupiscence and is the origin of a lack of peace in our interior life. When Christ greets the apostles in the Upper Room after He rises from the dead, He says twice: "Peace be with you" (John 20:19). This is not the absence of conflict but refers to the tranquility of order within the powers of the soul, blessed by healing grace.

Now, there are two movements by which this justification takes place. The first demands that a person, by his free will, loses the condition of sinfulness by being displeased with sin. If his displeasure with sin as an adult is imperfect—that is, if it is primarily a fear of punishment—he has what we call "attrition" or "imperfect contrition." While imperfect, this attrition is sufficient to open his soul to God's grace. If, on the other hand, his turning away from sin is motivated by a pure love of God, we say he has "perfect contrition" (CCC 1452–1453). The second movement or personal act in justification is the choice to love God. He has to have true affection for God, to enjoy God as someone with Whom he shares a true communion of life. He must love and desire the possibility of blessedness at the end of life by the indwelling of the Holy Spirit.

Justification, then, is a real interior change *and* a personal act— at least in anyone who has a free will. A baby, on the other hand, is justified by being baptized because there is not, and cannot be, any contrary act to the divine movement within the child. As we have said, though, as the baby grows older and becomes capable of acts of free will, he will need catechesis so that his grace will bear fruit—but it will also be necessary for him to begin to embrace this justification by being displeased with sin and by having affection for God. In adults, catechesis precedes justification; in infants it follows justification.

We can see this double movement in the baptismal rite, which includes three questions that are negative and three that are positive. In the three negative questions, the person is asked if he renounces Satan, and all his pomp, and all his worldly allurements, to which he answers "yes." This shows his displeasure with sin. In the second three questions, he is asked if he believes in the Trinity, among other articles of faith, to which he answers "yes." Justification, then, though it demands faith, is not by faith alone. It consists in, by faith, being displeased with sin and then, by faith and through the supernaturally infused gifts of the Holy Spirit, having affection for God. The preparation for justification may take place quickly (as in St. Paul) or over a long period of time (as in St. Augustine), but the actual change from being unrighteous to being righteous occurs in an instant, when a person accepts Christ and, following his Great Commission (Matt. 28:16–20), seeks Baptism.

Finally, justification consists both in a real conversion and the true forgiveness of sins, so that we are no longer vessels of sin or wrath but of faith and hope and charity. The justified one, in fact, is a new creation with divine life in him. Augustine says that the justified man is: "At one and the same time, both just and a sinner." Luther took this to mean that the soul in the state of grace was still *truly* a sinner but was considered just by God, who overlooked this evil. Aquinas and Augustine, however, meant that man was *truly* just but still had weaknesses after Baptism that tended to sin. This is expressed in the triple lust: "the lust of the flesh and the lust of the eyes and the pride of life" (1 John 2:16).

The justification of the human soul is the greatest work of God. That sounds like a huge claim, especially since God created everything out of nothing. Indeed, to bring something out of nothing is inconceivable to us mortal, limited beings who can only "create" with what is already present to us. So, purely as to the manner of action, we do have to say that Creation is God's greatest act.

Grace Explained

But the work of justification, in elevating the human will beyond its natural capabilities, is on the whole an even greater work. In the Creation of the universe, things arrived at *being*. In the justification, though, we arrive at *God*. This is why St. Thomas Aquinas says that one soul in the state of grace, from the point of view of the work that is done, is worth more than all the heavens and the earth put together, than all of nature seen in the movement of time.

Given this wonderful supernatural change, is justification a miracle? Genuine miracles have three characteristics. First, a miracle must occur by divine power; that is, there can be no power in nature that creates the miraculous occurrence. Second, a miracle must be completely beyond the power of the object being acted upon. For example, the resurrection of the dead always fulfills this criterion because there is no power whatsoever in a dead human body that can bring it back to life. Third, a miraculous action must occur in a manner contrary to the normal order in which such an action occurs in nature. For instance, Christ brought about some healings that could have occurred with medical care, but what makes His healings miraculous was that they occurred instantaneously simply by His word, without the slow, natural process of healing.

Applying these criteria to justification, first it is clear that this act of grace is truly divine. The second point is tricky, though. Is being filled with the presence of the Holy Trinity totally contrary or beyond the powers that are found in our nature? Sts. Augustine and Thomas Aquinas say that it is characteristic of mankind that we are "capable of God," which means that for our true human fulfillment we must enjoy divine intimacy. Therefore, it is in no sense an alienation of human nature to be elevated to this divine intimacy because man's natural home is not here but with God.

This is absolutely essential to understand. Because man has an intellect, his natural home is the vision of God. Anyone who can understand the relationship of one effect in this universe to one cause wants to know the first and primary explanation itself. And that can only be reached when, without mediation and thus by the light of God's glory itself, we enter into the mystery of God in Heaven. As Aquinas says; "Man by nature is called to an end by nature which he cannot attain by nature, but only by grace because of the exalted character of the end" (*Commentary on the* De Trinitate *of Boethius*, Q. 6, a. 4, reply to obj. 5. cf. *Summa Theologica*, I–II, q. 5, art. 5, ad 1; *De Veritate*, 22, 7).

Of course, this does not mean that we're naturally capable of moving ourselves to know God as He is in Himself. We're not even naturally capable of being receptive to this movement, in the sense that we do not need God's aid to prepare ourselves. But what it does mean is that once God begins to move us in this supernatural way, we finally come home. We no longer feel alienated in this world because living without this intimacy, without the ability to truly adopt God's will as our own, is the source of our alienation. This is not about gritting our teeth and slavishly doing the will of another; rather, just as friends come to love what their friends love, so, too, the more in love we become with God the more we appreciate what He is doing in the world as a whole and with us as individuals.

Finally, in the third sense of the miraculous, sometimes justification is accomplished according to the order of nature, through a slow process of preparation. But at other times—again, St. Paul is the iconic example—God accomplishes this preparation by instantaneously disposing someone to receive His gift when he was not disposed previously. God is not limited by the natural process in which a nature is perfected, and He does not act against the nature of the person or thing in doing this. Rather, He is acting beyond nature, which would fulfill the third criterion of the miraculous. Thus, justification is not strictly speaking miraculous because the second of the three criteria is missing.

Grace Explained

Aristotle begins his *Metaphysics* with the statement: "All men by nature desire to know." This can only be perfected in the vision of God after death. How can we say that we are not valued? How can we feel that we are alone? How can we feel that no one cares for us? How can we spend our lives wasting time in pursuits that bring nothing to our spirits, such as the unbridled pursuit of pleasure and wealth? How can we spend our time destroying people so we can get ahead? We are created for nothing less than to experience the very interior life of God Himself on earth, and to know the Beloved in Himself as He is in Heaven! When that baptismal water was poured over our head, we entered into the wonder of God; we experienced union with the greatest act that God has performed, the glorification of God in Christ dying on the Cross and rising from the dead. How can we feel that we're not appreciated and loved, when God has loved us enough to elevate us to share His own mysteries with us?

Chapter 13

Merit

It is now time to talk about the last effect of God's movement in our souls: merit, which is the effect of cooperating grace. In operating grace, God moves us and we freely receive His movement, which is partaking of His nature. God works *in* us. But in cooperating grace, God moves us; we receive His movement; and then we participate in the movement of our souls in a divine way. We move our free will, filled with divine love and divine truth, in accordance with the grace and will of God. God works *with* us.

In this way, the good deeds we perform are enlivened by divine charity. As time goes on and we increasingly embrace this cooperation, we become more and more consumed with the desire to be in Heaven and to see God in the face. At the same time, all our everyday works are done from God's point of view. Friends love what their friends love; God is our friend and so we see things from a supernatural point of view.

Some theologians have maintained that the only really meritorious action is to accept Christ at the moment of death. But our perseverance in the moment of death is determined in part by our actions and habits throughout our lives. It is true that a person can convert at the hour of death after a lifetime of wickedness, but it is certainly not something to count on. How we carry on in the ordinary things of life prepares us for Heaven.

Grace Explained

Now, it's very important to understand precisely what we mean by "merit." Christ told His apostles, "So you also, when you have done all that is commanded you, say, 'We are unworthy servants; we have only done what was our duty'" (Luke 17:10). We can never presume that we deserve the ultimate gift of the vision of God, and we cannot merit it from Him, at least in strict equivalence. Remember, before God there is no boasting. Even the grace of final perseverance is something that our works cannot merit; even the saints must pray for it daily: "And lead us not into temptation, but deliver us from evil." And, "God come to my assistance [operating grace]; Lord make haste to help me [cooperating grace]" (variation on Ps. 70:1, which is often prayed during the Church's daily Liturgy of the Hours, e.g., in Morning Prayer).

At the same time, it's clear in Scripture that there is a connection between our actions here on earth and our eternal reward: "Then the King will say to those at his right hand, 'Come, O blessed of my Father, inherit the kingdom prepared for you from the foundation of the world.... Truly, I say to you, as you did it to one of the least of these my brethren, you did it to me'" (Matt. 25:34, 40). And so there are true and proper consequences that the just (or the unjust) merit for themselves according to the manner in which they have allowed God to move them. Since God works with us, in every meritorious act there are two who act together: the Holy Spirit and the person himself.

The first divine movement within us that enlivens our souls to follow God comes from Him alone and cannot be merited. But, as we have said, the God who created you without you will not redeem you without you; your particular participation in this work is what brings forth merit. We cannot merit grace, but we can merit Heaven.

In Catholic theology, all merit is divided into two types: congruent and condign. This respects the manner in which one becomes worthy of repayment for a service rendered. Condign merit is *quid pro quo* among equals. It is based on strict equivalence: I buy a loaf of bread and I owe the seller a just price. This cannot take place with God. He is infinite; we are not. There can be no demand for justice for our works from God.

Congruent merit is not strict equivalence between equals but an example of proportionate equality. God accepts that the person has done what he is able to do given the limitations of his nature and rewards him not because his actions are strictly worthy of God, but because he has chosen to cooperate with grace. It is not that our acts of free will cause God to reward us, but that He chooses to condescend to reward us for doing the best we can. He is saying, in effect, "I never condemn those who do what I ask of them; since I never act against human nature, I reward based on human nature." God promised to reward us and His promise is infallible.

But there is also a part of our action that is worthy of merit in strict equivalence, and that is the part that is the direct result of the movement of the Holy Spirit. Remember that both we and God act in our good works. The merit received as a result of our allowing the Holy Spirit to act in us is called condign merit. This is the reward given strictly according to the order of justice as the deed merits—not from our cooperation with grace but to the extent that we have become, in a sense, transparent to the movement of the Spirit. In other words, God rewards two in any meritorious act: Himself and the individual who acts.

Our participation in and cooperation with God's action allows us to say that we can merit eternal life. Indeed, that's the whole purpose of choosing our actions and behaviors and habits. We participate in the realization of our destiny. By the manner in which we love on earth, we prepare ourselves to be with the One Whom we love in Heaven. It is not by our actions and deeds as such, however, but by the extent to which they are moved by divine love, that we can be said to receive the just reward of our labors at the end of our lives. It does not matter if our deeds are grand or simple, so long as they come from love. I often ask Catholics if they know the principle by which we merit Heaven, for in His house He has many mansions. Many say that it is the difficulty of the work that determines our status in Heaven. Actually, it is the love with which the work is done, no matter how humble the tasks.

Consider the Blessed Virgin. After conceiving Christ in her womb, what was the first thing she did to show her divine love? Did she go out and write a newspaper column, or start a business, or try to rule a nation? No, she went to help her cousin Elizabeth, who was with child in her old age. In the Visitation, we see the practical charity of the Blessed Virgin Mary and the divine love exhibited in a very simple action, an action that was the basis for the composition of one of the greatest religious songs ever: "The Magnificat" (Luke 1:46–55). We can see this spirituality also in St. Thérèse of Lisieux, "the Little Flower." She understood that the strength of her acts came not from their worldly greatness but from the love with which they were performed.

One beautiful truth about grace and merit is that, while we can't merit the grace of our own first conversion, we can merit it for others. In our prayers, we often invoke the merits of the Blessed Virgin Mary and the saints. For example, priests may add at the end of the Confession rite:

> May the Passion of Our Lord Jesus Christ, the merits of the Blessed Virgin Mary and of all the saints and also whatever good you do or evil you endure be cause for the remission of your sins, the increase of grace, and the reward of life everlasting.

God responds to the prayers of the saints by congruent merit, that is, by a union of friendship and mercy. As friends respond to the requests of friends, so God responds through a union of love to the requests of those who are His friends. And so as long as the person whose conversion we're trying to bring does not put a block in the way—by a strong movement of their free will against grace—it's possible for the saints and the Blessed Virgin and even for ourselves to be the cause of his conversion. St. Thomas Aquinas says that if we love God and He loves us, that if we do His will, in a certain sense it is a fittingly friendly thing for God to want to do man's will. This is especially true in meritorious prayer.

Here's an important question for those with modern views on religion: are temporal goods influenced by merit? That is, do we merit good things (or bad things) here on earth from our love of God? People often feel that they are unloved by God because they lack temporal goods. Historically, for instance, some Calvinists believed that wealth represented holiness—that is to say, merit with the Lord—while poverty was a sign of reprobation. Protestant evangelists today often make reference to the "Prosperity Gospel." But the whole purpose of this book has been to say that there's only one good that matters in the final analysis, and that is seeing God in the face. To the extent that temporal goods, at a particular moment in our lives, set the conditions that make it possible to progress in holiness, then you could say perhaps they do fall under grace and merit. But a person who is filled with grace can make at least as much use of suffering, in his growth in cooperating with the Lord, as he would with all the temporal goods in the world. Very often, in fact, these goods aren't good for us because we become distracted by worldly success and forget our final purpose—and the One Whom we must rely on to get there.

The grace of God is more necessary to us than food and drink; it moves us to prepare ourselves for our true home. For we have here no abiding city; we are only pilgrims on the way (see Heb. 13:14). How sad it is that so many people today seem not to realize, or even to desire, their true destiny: the vision of God. How sad it is that we have lowered our horizons to materialism, striving after the best gadgets and promotions and pleasures, a return to the ancient, pagan, pre-Christian world. How sick and how dark this view of human dignity is! How unrealistic to sacrifice the spiritual for the temporal!

When we lower our standards and our desires like this, it becomes easy to define religion down — say to a political program, or just to feeling good about yourself. We think we can do anything we want as long as we're nice. I don't mean to alarm you, but you can be nice and still lose your soul. What we are called to is something so much greater: to be elevated to a divine point of view, to allow the active gifts of the Holy Spirit to change us from within, making us true children of God. We will only have a truly human face, with which to regard and transform the world, when God can look into our hearts — as a refiner does into the crucible — and see His own image.

☞

I wrote this book to show you what blessings Catholicism reveals to the believer. First is the blessing of existence itself. Second is the reality of the human intellect that is able to be elevated to partake of God's divine nature. Third, and most important, is that the believer—by faith—can be so elevated right here on earth through entering a loving exchange of hearts with Christ, and then in Heaven by actually realizing human nature through the final knowledge of God.

I have encouraged you to look to the supernatural order, to acquire the supernatural point of view as the fullest expression of what it means to be human. That doesn't mean that all the things we do here on earth aren't good and valuable; but they are not our final purpose, and they will not fulfill our souls. The final value of our worldly deeds can only be seen and understood in allowing God to take over our lives—not against our free will but in free cooperation with His will for us in all the little and big things of every day. In so doing, we will also be sorrowful and contrite when we sin, and we will consult Him and His mercy in using our personal gifts in all our actions.

The justification of man does not consist in what he does, nor in how consistent or successful he is. The justification of man consists in union with the Holy Spirit and in allowing that Spirit to transform his point of view by elevating his soul to God.

~

About the Author

Fr. Brian Thomas Becket Mullady is the son of an Air Force officer and was raised throughout the United States. He entered the Dominican Order in 1966 and was ordained in Oakland, California, in 1972. He has been a parish priest, high school teacher, retreat master, mission preacher, and university professor. He received his doctorate in sacred theology (STD) from the Angelicum University in Rome and was a professor there for six years. He has taught at several colleges and seminaries in the United States. He is currently a mission preacher and retreat master for the Western Dominican Province. Fr. Mullady has had fourteen series on the EWTN Global Catholic Network and appears weekly on EWTN Radio's *Open Line*. He is the author of four books and numerous articles and writes the answer column in *Homiletic and Pastoral Review*. He is also designated as an official Missionary of Mercy by Pope Francis.